MAKE MONEY READING BOOKS

How to Start and Operate Your Own Home-Based Freelance Reading Service

Bruce Fife

PICCADILLY BOOKS
COLORADO SPRINGS, COLORADO

Piccadilly Books
P.O. Box 25203
Colorado Springs, CO 80936

Library of Congress Cataloging-in-Publication Data

Fife, Bruce, 1952-
   Make money reading books: how to start and operate your own
   home-based freelance reading service / by Bruce Fife.
        p.   cm.
   Includes bibliographical references and index.
   ISBN 0-941599-20-5
   1. Literateurs.   2. Editors.   3. Reading--Vocational guidance.
   4. Self-employed.   I. Title.
PN151.F45 1993
070.5'1'02373--dc20   92-26184
                                                      CIP

Cover design by Robin Axtell

Printed in the United States of America

CONTENTS

Foreword   5

1   Making Money Reading   7

2   Freelance Reading Opportunities   11

3   Setting Up Your Business   25

4   Marketing Your Services   33

5   Guidelines for Success   50

6   How to Become a Published Author   58

7   Literary Services   85

8   Book Reviewing   115

9   Researching   130

10 Translating   141

11 Indexing   153

12 Literary Representation   162

13 Manuscript Reading   176

14 Other Reading Jobs   187

Appendix: Resources   194

Index   206

FOREWORD

When I read the manuscript for *Make Money Reading Books* I knew it would be an invaluable resource for people who love to read and would like to make money in their own home-based business. It is extremely informative and very well-written. The author, Bruce Fife, has years of experience with books, as a publisher, editor, consultant, and teacher. In one way or another he's been involved with all of the things that he writes about in the book and has been very successful.

I know this to be true because I run my own freelance business, Blue Sky Literary Services, and I've had numerous rewarding experiences working with him. He is a professional and knows the subject that he has written about. I give him credit for not keeping the wisdom of his experience and success to himself.

I first met the author when I was starting out, in one of the many classes that he has taught over the years on writing and publishing. He helped me on my way and always seemed to have the answers to my questions.

Make Money Reading Books will have the answers for you too. It is a comprehensive, easy-to-read book that will allow you to jump right into the world of publishing and begin an exciting career as a freelance reader. But not only does Mr. Fife thoroughly cover the variety of exciting ways to make money reading, he also shows you the business side of setting up your own business, marketing yourself, and achieving success.

Do you want to work full-time or part-time making money as a reader? Do you need to learn how to find clients and how you can work out of your home? *Make Money Reading Books* provides thorough, easy-to-understand answers to these questions and many more. Chapter by chapter, Mr. Fife gives you the benefit of his years of experience as a book publisher, editor, and consultant.

Up until now, you had to take one of his classes to learn how to make money in the world of print. Now that Mr. Fife has taken the time to craft out a book that covers in great detail all of those areas in the publishing profession where one can make money, his experience and insight are open to us all. His book is packed full of hard-earned wisdom. Read it, and you'll be well on your way to success making money reading books.

Edward Keneski
Blue Sky Literary Services

CHAPTER 1

MAKING MONEY READING

Are you one of those people who loves to spend free time reading? Would you find pleasure relaxing in your favorite easy chair cuddled up to a captivating novel? Do you enjoy browsing through bookstores or checking out new books on the best seller list? If so, then this book could open up a whole new world of opportunity for you.

For many people, reading is an enjoyable, leisurely activity. An activity most people would do more often if not burdened with other responsibilities. But what if you could earn money while you were reading? What if you could earn enough money to make reading a lucrative part-time business, or even a full-time career? Just imagine a job that would pay you to read books, plays, magazine articles, and other materials. As a freelance reader, there would be no boss looking over your shoulder, telling you what to do, or when to come to work. You work your own hours in your own home.

Would you like such a job? Who wouldn't, right? But you might be saying to yourself, no such job exists. As incredible as it may sound to you, this type of job does indeed exist. If you like to read and are a good reader, you can become a professional reader.

This is a completely legitimate income opportunity enjoyed by many home-based workers all over the country. Several different types of freelance reading jobs are available, each having a different purpose and function. For the most part, these are not obscure or off-beat jobs, but established career opportunities available to anyone.

If you are one of those people who loves to read, here is an opportunity for you to get paid for doing something you enjoy. You wouldn't have to feel guilty about delaying a few household chores to relax and spend a couple of hours reading because you will be earning some extra cash and enjoying yourself at the same time.

The question you might be asking yourself now is: Who would pay somebody to read? My answer: Lots of people. I do, for one. I am a publisher for an independent book publishing company. Everything our company publishes is read by independent readers. There is a huge and growing market for competent readers in the publishing industry and in the business world in general.

I send out checks to people we work with continuously. Although the amount readers can earn depends on the client and the type of reading done, in our case, reading a single manuscript could earn the reader anywhere from $50 to $500 or more. Extensive or detailed jobs could pay as much as $5000! Hourly payments can be as much as $50 or more, although more typically they are around $7-$20.

The readers we use are scattered all across the country. Location is no problem. We work with out of town readers as easily as those we hire locally. For those who are out of town, we simply correspond through the mail. We send them manuscripts, and they work on them at home and return the material to us when they are finished. It's that simple. It is a mutually beneficial business relationship.

The world is becoming more and more dependent on the written word. Look, for example, at the number of books in print. Hundreds of thousands of different books are in print. In fact, over 50,000 new books are published every year! This number is rapidly increasing with the growing popularity of self-publishing and increasing number of small presses coming into existence.

All unpublished manuscripts contain mistakes in spelling, grammar, punctuation, and the like. In the process of preparing manuscripts for publication, typographical errors can also be introduced. Before a manuscript is published, these errors must be corrected. Usually, several proofreaders and editors examine the material prior to publication. In the past, most of the editing and proofreading was done by employees of the publishing company, but more and more of this type of work is being done by freelancers.

Looking for errors in unpublished manuscripts is only one of the jobs readers are hired to do. Readers are also used to evaluate books and screenplays for book clubs, film producers, and others. Some readers provide book summaries or reviews to newspaper, magazine, and book publishers. Others search for certain types of data in the material they read, while some don't do anything except just read. Readers are hired for many different types of jobs, but the primary function of all readers is to read.

Publishing companies are only one of the industries that uses readers. Many businesses, as well as individuals, use readers. For this reason, the job opportunities are limitless. There will always be a need for reading services as described in this book, and this need is rapidly growing.

In this book, you will learn about the many different types of reading opportunities available to you. You will learn what skills are needed for each job, how to develop these skills, how much you can expect to earn, how to go about finding this type of work, and how to set up and operate a successful reading service out of your home. You will learn how to turn reading into a profitable business.

The purpose of this book is to show you how to take advantage of the legitimate opportunities that exist in providing freelance reading services. You will also learn how to avoid the many unethical practices devised by con artists that claim to offer similar opportunities.

Most of the reading services I describe in this book traditionally have been performed by those in the writing profession. Being a writer, however, is certainly not a requirement and in most cases average writing skill is all that is necessary. The term *reader* is used since the primary function of those who perform these services is not writing but reading, although some writing may be required. Some of the reading services I describe are well-known professions not typically referred to by this term, but by specific titles such as *proofreader, copy editor,* or *reviewer.* In some cases there is no recognized title or term, but in order to distinguish them from other readers I have given them a descriptive name such as *student reader, clipping service reader,* and *article reader.* I have used the term *reader* in a general sense in reference to all of the reading services mentioned in this book. In the following chapter I will identify each of the different types of readers and describe the services they provide.

CHAPTER 2

FREELANCE READING OPPORTUNITIES

WHO HIRES READERS?

In this section you will discover where to market your services as a freelance reader. As you will see, there is a great demand for qualified readers. Many people and businesses are actively seeking the types of services you can provide.

Publishers

The most obvious job market for readers is with publishing companies. Newspaper, book, and magazine publishers all use readers to some degree for editing, proofreading, fact finding, indexing, and other reading services. They routinely hire people to provide these services for them. Large publishing companies hire full-time editors to perform most of these functions. However, many medium and small publishing companies employ freelance readers. The real job opportunities for freelance readers is not with the giant publishing houses but with the medium and small or independent publishers.

With the explosion of the self-publishing and the small press industry over the past few years, the need for freelance readers has mushroomed. Small publishing companies and self-publishers cannot afford to hire full-time editors and readers so they rely heavily on independent workers.

There are literally thousands of small publishing companies in operation throughout the country. An exact figure cannot be named because the number increases daily. Many of these companies are large enough to be included in trade directories such as *Literary Market Place* and *Writer's Market*. *Writer's Market* lists about 700 book publishers and over 3000 magazine publishers. This is a huge market for potential readers. There are many more times that number which are not listed. These are very small publishing companies and self-publishers.

Books and magazines produced, without the aid of readers, by very small publishing companies and particularly self-published material are prone to contain an unusually large number of spelling, grammar, and other errors. The people who produce these materials desperately need the help of freelance readers.

Over the past few years many excellent self-published books have been published. These have been properly edited and proofread, most likely by freelancers. The appearance of several best selling books on self-publishing and the easy availability of computers and desktop publishing systems have made self-publishing extremely popular. The number of self-publishers are increasing phenomenally, thus providing new opportunities to freelance readers.

Writers

Publishing companies are only a small part of the market available to readers. Writers and other individuals are also in need of readers and are willing to pay for their services. In fact, writers provide an even bigger potential market for freelance readers than publishers. Although publishers produce thousands of books and magazines every year, all of the material they produce comes from writers. There are many more writers than there are publishers.

The competition to sell manuscripts to publishers is fierce. I would estimate that less than one percent of the material sent to publishers is ever published. Since so much material is being written, publishers can be very selective. The material they choose to publish must not only have commercial value, but be very competently written and free of editing and factual errors. Any manuscript that contains errors stands little chance at being accepted for publication. Most publishers will not want to waste time with writers whose material contains too many mistakes. I have heard of some editors who will reject a manuscript if it contains a single spelling or grammatical error.

Most published authors know the value of good editing and use readers frequently. Inexperienced writers are also recognizing the advantage of using independent readers. Those who do use readers greatly increase their chances of selling what they write.

Not only are editing and proofreading services valuable to writers, but so are critiquing, research, translation, literary, and other services. The services of any of these readers can make the writer's material more salable.

Students and Educators

Another huge market for freelance readers is with students and teachers. Colleges and universities provide a source of thousands of potential clients who are continually writing reports, theses, dissertations, and term papers. The attraction of polishing student's material and hopefully improving their grades makes your services very enticing. All students are potential clients—whether they are undergraduates or graduates. Even instructors who work under the strain of a "publish or perish" philosophy can use your services. I have read doctoral dissertations that have contained *hundreds* of spelling, grammar, and typographical errors. The fact that some students have had eight or more years of college does not mean they can write clearly and accurately.

You are not limited to local schools. You can approach students and faculty from any university or college through the mail. This opens up an enormous client potential that renews itself every year, providing you a never ending source of customers.

Businesses

Any business is a potential customer. A great deal of writing is done by executives, staff, salespeople, and researchers as part of their job. They write reports, flyers, brochures, and catalogs in additon to publishing studies, creating advertisements, and composing letters. All of these materials require somebody to edit, proofread, and prepare them for publication or distribution. These people are not generally professional writers, nor are they trained to edit the material properly. Can you imagine the embarrassment of a business owner who misspells a key word in a $10,000 advertisement placed in a magazine? Or typographical errors in a brochure which tries to convince customers they have the skill and talent to do a good job and deserve your business? How competent are they if their brochure is full of errors?

Many larger businesses have marketing and advertising departments or public relations departments. Some have their own in-house editorial or publishing departments. These departments produce a great deal of written material. Whether a company has a trained writing staff or not, they all can use the services of freelance readers.

Government

Federal, state, county, and city government offices all across the country are potential customers. There are over 43,000 government offices in the United States. The federal government spends over $200 million a year for goods and services supplied by vendors and contractors, many of whom are self-employed freelancers supplying writing, editorial, and reading services.

Like businesses, governments produce technical manuals, training manuals, catalogs, newsletters, policy manuals, reports, news releases, public relations material, and brochures. They have a great need for readers.

I have mentioned that publishers are a prime market for readers, but the Government Printing Office is by far the largest producer of books and pamphlets in the United States.

Non-Profit Organizations and Associations

Non-profit organizations, clubs, and associations also provide a large market for readers. They, too, produce many of the same types of materials as businesses and governments. Many of these organizations produce their own newsletters and magazines, and even publish books and catalogs.

Since many of the organizations are run and operated by volunteers or non-professionals, they desire and need the services readers can offer. Readers help make their materials more professional looking and competent. Many of these organizations don't realize they even need reading services, but will recognize the need when contacted.

When you come right down to it, almost every business, organization, and individual is a potential client. You are not limited to your local area. Because you work through the mail, you can even provide services to those in other countries. In reality, the world is your market.

TYPES OF FREELANCE READERS

In this section I will briefly describe several different types of readers and their functions. Most reading jobs require not only reading, but some type of writing. This could be correcting errors in a text, adding to it, checking it, or summarizing or reviewing it. Some of these jobs are in high demand while others have relatively limited potential for anything more than part-time work. Frequently, the jobs and functions of some reading services overlap. Many readers offer clients services involving several of the functions discussed in this chapter. Being willing and able to do several different reading jobs makes you more versatile, provides you with more opportunities for work, and makes you more valuable to clients. You may specialize in any one category, or branch out with services in two or more.

More detailed information on each of the following is given in individual chapters.

Proofreader

The proofreader's primary job is to look for and correct typographical errors, and errors in spelling, grammar, punctuation, and the like. A college degree in English is most desirable, but not required.

Anything which is put into writing and meant for other people to read should be proofread. Most frequently people use employees, friends, and colleagues as proofreaders, usually because they are cheap or free. These people can often catch most obvious errors and make the work somewhat presentable. However, a professional proofreader will do a much better job. A proofreader's services are of value to almost any type of business. All businesses have advertising flyers, catalogs, sales literature, and brochures. These all should be proofread before publication and distribution. The writer, although he may be competent, will not catch all errors. Publishers hire proofreaders because they know that even editors make mistakes, as do typists. Proofreading provides the final check before publication.

Copy Editor

There are many different types of editors, each performing distinct functions. They include assistant editors, executive editors, managing editors, and production editors, to name just a few. The copy editor's function is to proofread, correct errors, and improve writing mechanics. Frequently, copy editors as well as the other types of editors, are all referred to simply as editors.

Copyediting encompasses more than proofreading. Copy editors correct typographical, spelling, grammar, and punctuation errors, as well as improve sentence structure and thought flow. They will rewrite phrases or sentences, if necessary, to make an idea clearer or to make the reading flow smoother.

Editing requires a good knowledge of basic English grammar and structure. A bachelor's degree in English would be expected and a graduate degree highly preferred. Occasionally, advanced degrees in other fields are acceptable, if you can show competence.

If you have the necessary skills to be a good copy editor, it can be a lucrative and rewarding part-time endeavor or full-time career.

Technical Reader

Technical readers may be editors or proofreaders. Technical readers are usually people who have training, education, or extensive experience in some particular specialized field. These types of readers are used to edit and proofread technical works such as college textbooks or scientific studies. Readers look for accuracy and consistency with established known research in manuscripts and reports that are of a technical nature. The books may be technical texts such as *Introduction to Biology,* or general interest works on a somewhat technical subject such as *How to Be Fit and Healthy.*

Technical readers are required to have advanced college degrees—preferably a Ph.D. in the subject matter being reviewed. For some topics, formal education is less important than actual experience. For example, a book on sailing, gold mining, cooking, or carpentry would best be reviewed by someone who has had extensive experience in these endeavors rather than a college degree. If you have an advanced college degree or can be considered an authority in some field, you could work as a technical reader.

Literary Critic

One of the primary reasons book and magazine publishers cite for rejecting manuscripts is poor or inadequate writing ability. Many of these works could be improved and become publishable if the authors have them critiqued by another person. Frequently, writers overlook weaknesses in their own writing which can be pointed out and corrected by someone else.

A literary critic can offer a novice writer valuable criticism and suggestions for improvement, thus greatly enhancing the author's chances for publication. The literary critic will read a manuscript and then write the author a detailed, honest evaluation of the work. The critic will point out weaknesses, stress strengths, and make suggestions for improvement. Any type of material can be critiqued: nonfiction and fiction book-length manuscripts, magazine articles, essays, or school or business reports.

No special schooling or training is required to become a literary critic, although experience as a teacher or writer, or having a college degree in English or literature, is highly recommended.

Book Reviewer

A freelance book reviewer reads books and writes short reviews for newspapers and magazines. Although most publications have in-house book editors or people to write or review books, many publications buy book reviews from freelance reviewers. If you have a love for reading, this is an excellent opportunity to earn extra cash. As a book reviewer, you can read a wide variety of books which are of interest to you in the privacy of your own home. You choose the types of books you want to review. Usually, the publisher will send you a free review copy for this purpose. After reading the book, you write a short, concise review describing the book and expressing your opinion on its strengths and weaknesses.

No particular education is required, but a college degree is helpful, particularly in English and, to a lesser extent, history or political science since many popular books nowadays touch on these subjects. Some reviewers specialize in specific fields such as sociology, medicine, earth science, and such, and a college degree or special training would be necessary. Your primary skill as a reviewer, however, would be the ability to comprehend the material you read and express your thoughts effectively in writing. A beginner can get a good feel for what makes good reviews by studying published reviews. Read the book reviews contained in large circulation newspapers such as the *New York Times*, *Chicago Tribune*, and *The Los Angeles Times*. They can be located in your local public library.

Researcher

A researcher collects information and checks facts on particular subjects for clients. The subjects could range from finding information about the evolution and development of the yo-yo, to finding the latest statistics on unemployment. Writers, publishers, students, teachers, and business people all use the services of researchers to help them find information for speeches, presentations, seminars, reports, studies, articles, or books. The clients may not have the time or the know-how to get the type of information needed. So, they hire freelance researchers.

A college degree is not mandatory, but researchers typically have degrees in library science. The library science curriculum teaches students the resources available in libraries and how to access them. You don't need a degree to be an effective researcher, but taking an appropriate library science class or two will greatly enhance your understanding of the materials and resources available.

To be a good researcher you must like to read and enjoy the challenge of locating often obscure information. In some respects, researching is like detective work, and you must search for the clues to solve the mystery, which is to locate information for the client. It can be exciting work and it can be mundane, depending on the subject. Most of your research will be done in the quiet setting of your local library. Although you can use interlibrary loan to get materials from other libraries, having a large public or college library available to work in will allow you to do a better job.

Translator

Translators read and convert written materials from one language into another. Freelance translators can work at home on their own time schedule. Their biggest challenge is accurately expressing thoughts and ideas from one language into another.

Many companies which do business outside the country need the services of translators. Publishers use them to translate books and magazine articles into foreign languages for marketing abroad. There is a strong demand for translation work of technical and scientific materials from government and business, as well as publishers.

Most translators have college degrees in one or more foreign languages, or English if they are from a non-English speaking country. Although a college degree isn't mandatory, fluency in the foreign language is. Additional college language classes can also be beneficial in sharpening skills. Translators can become accredited with the American Translators Association. The association requires a competency test for accreditation. Those who are accredited are listed in the association's registry of translators, which is used by prospective clients to locate translators. Being an accredited translator indicates competency and is a strong selling point to potential clients.

Indexer

Another type of job most people are unaware of is that of the indexer. The indexer creates the index found in the back of many nonfiction books. Publishers and other businesses use freelance indexers to create these indexes.

Once a book has been edited and laid out in final format, an indexer reads it, noting certain words and the pages they are on. He then compiles this word list in alphabetical order and returns it with the manuscript to the client. Tens of thousands of new books are published each year, many of which have indexes prepared by freelancers. As the small press industry begins to grow, the need for indexers will also increase.

If you like to read and don't mind taking notes as you do, then you can easily become an indexer. There are no education, training, or certification requirements. In fact, the basics of the job can be learned in a relatively short time. Many home-based careers require professional skills that take hours of study and practice to develop. Indexing, however, is one of those rare jobs where the basics can be learned in a relatively short amount of time. If you can read well, you can be an indexer.

Literary Agent

Approximately 400,000 book-length manuscripts are written and sent to publishers every year. The majority of these manuscripts are submitted over and over to a variety of publishers in hopes of making a sale. For this reason, publishers are overwhelmed with material to evaluate. The vast majority of unsolicited manuscripts sent to publishers are either unmarketable or so poorly written that they are never accepted for publication. Literary agents provide a valuable service to publishers by screening out unpublishable manuscripts. In fact, more and more of the large publishing companies are refusing to accept unsolicited manuscripts. All material they receive must be submitted by an agent or it won't even be considered. For this reason, the need for good literary agents is increasing. Some literary agents work for agencies, but most are independent freelancers working out of a private office or their home.

Agents spend most of their time reading manuscripts. They evaluate the manuscript's chances for success in getting published. If they feel a writer has written a marketable manuscript, they will represent the author and his work by actively seeking a publisher to publish it.

The agent will prepare and send out query letters and book proposals, and instruct the author on how to properly prepare the manuscript. If a sale is made, the agent receives a commission of about 15 percent on royalties paid to the author. Frequently, agents also charge consulting and reading fees. Since many of the manuscripts agents read will not be suitable for representation, they charge the authors for time spent reading. In this case, the agent is literally paid to read and nothing more. However, the financial reward from earning commissions is much greater and the goal of the agent is to identify salable material and then find it a publisher.

A love for reading is definitely a requirement for a literary agent since he must read many manuscripts in search of those which meet his standards for representation. No particular training or schooling is needed to be a literary agent. What is needed is a knowledge of what can and can't sell, and how to properly submit material to publishers and negotiate a publishing agreement. All of this can be learned by experience and through books currently in print. Experience is the best teacher and the more experience an agent has, the better he or she becomes.

Manuscript Reader

Book publishers receive multitudes of unsolicited manuscripts daily. Editors have little time to spend on this material so they assign this task to junior editors or hire *first readers*. Although these editors sift through all unsolicited manuscripts, they concentrate on looking for those manuscripts with the most promise. These editors can tell after reading just a page or two whether a manuscript should be rejected (as most are) or should receive more careful consideration and further reading.

Some publishers, rather than use their employees, will hire freelance manuscript readers to read those works which show some promise. The publisher will assign the freelancer to read the material and write a brief summary and critical evaluation. From this book report, the senior editor will determine if they should reject the manuscript or consider it more seriously. Manuscripts usually are read by many editors before they are eventually accepted for publication.

A college education is not necessary to be a manuscript reader. The primary requirements are good reading skills and the ability to evaluate the literary quality and marketability of a book.

Student Reader

This is one of those special opportunities you rarely hear about. A college education is not needed and no special training or experience is necessary. The only requirement is the ability to read well.

A student reader's job is to read books to students, usually college students who have physical handicaps which limit their reading ability. Students who are visually impaired need people to read their school assignments to them. So, colleges hire readers to help students with their education. Many colleges and universities offer this type of program to their handicapped students.

Clipping Service Reader

Many businesses and individuals seek articles written about them or on certain topics regarding their business, in newspapers and magazines. These articles help them in their publicity campaigns, which help promote their business or profession. With the multitude of publications being printed, it is a difficult task to monitor them all. For this reason, they hire a clipping service. The clipping service pays readers to search periodicals and look specifically for anything regarding the clients and their companies. Many of these readers are scattered around the country, reading both local and national publications.

You can be hired by a clipping service company to provide this service. No education is required and no special skills are necessary. Being willing and able to read regularly are the only requirements.

Article Reader

There are many national magazines which will reprint interesting articles from smaller publications. Readers who spot appropriate articles in local publications and send them to national magazines will be paid a finder's fee if the article is reprinted. Payments vary up to about $300 for a single article.

Not all magazines pay for finding articles which they reprint, and some don't reprint material from other sources. You must find those publications which do and learn what type of material they will accept.

Since the work depends entirely on your ability to spot appropriate articles and send them to the right buyer, no special education or skill is required. In fact, you don't even need to be able to read that well. If you can recognize an appropriate article when you see it, that is all the skill it takes.

SUMMARY

As you can see from this chapter, freelance readers have many job opportunities. College degrees are helpful but in many cases not necessary. The ability to read well and a love for reading are the primary prerequisites. As you have seen, most of the reading jobs require some additional work other than just reading. Knowledge in creative writing, English grammar and mechanics, publishing, and other academic fields can greatly enhance your chances for success.

In Chapters 3, 4, and 5, I explain how to set up your home-based reading business, how to market your services, and provide you with instructions on making your new business a success.

Some readers can enhance their chances for success by being published authors. For this reason, I provide details on how you can easily get published. In Chapter 6, I reveal the secrets of how a person with no publishing experience and only average writing skill can become a published author. These are tricks to the trade that even many writers don't know much about.

The rest of the chapters in this book are devoted to describing in detail the jobs and functions of each of the reading services mentioned in this chapter. Chapter 7 covers literary services, which include proofreading, copyediting, technical reading, and literary criticism services. Chapters 8, 9, 10, 11, 12, and 13 describe book reviewing, researching, translating, indexing, literary representation, and manuscript reading services respectively.

Student readers, clipping service readers, and magazine readers are described in Chapter 14. These last three are grouped together because the opportunities available in these jobs are much more limited than in any of the other services mentioned. Also included in this last chapter is a section on how con artists are using some of these reading services to swindle people out of their money—information you should be aware of.

The appendix provides many invaluable resources where readers can get additional information regarding each of the freelance reading services. It also includes marketing resources and professional guidance and instruction through magazines, books, and associations.

CHAPTER 3

SETTING UP YOUR BUSINESS

Before you begin operating as a freelance reader, you need to set up your business according to local and state laws. Since you are selling your services to clients as a reader, you are going into business just as any other business does and you are subject to the same laws and regulations as other businesses.

BUSINESS NAME

In setting up your business, your first consideration is choosing a name you will do business under. You may simply use your own name, or you can use your name or a part of your name in combination with some descriptive term such as "Mary Smith, Freelance Editor" or "Jones Indexing Services." You may also choose a name unrelated to your own given name, such as "Red Pencil Services" or "Quick Edit."

If you use any name other than just your first and last name, you must go to your local county courthouse and file for a fictitious name statement. The county officer will give you the legal right to do business under your chosen business name. They will also do a check on the name you have chosen to make sure no one else is already doing business under that name. If someone else is using that name, you must choose another. Believe it or not, you may think you have dreamed up a clever, original name only to find someone else is already using it or something very similar. I've heard many horror stories of two businesses with similar names getting mail, bills, and payments mixed up and having difficulty straightening the mess out. It is surprising how often people dream up what they believe are original names, only to be disappointed when they find them already in use. So, you may want to choose a couple of names just in case your first choice is unavailable.

Some states also require new businesses to get a business license or permit. You can check with your local state and city government to see what is required in your area.

BUSINESS ADDRESS

Your next consideration is choosing your mailing address. You can use your home address or you can rent a post office box. You may also rent a private postal box. Some people like to keep their business mail separate from personal mail. Also, if they live in an apartment or move frequently, a post office box provides more stability. Some people do not like to use a post office box because they feel it appears less legitimate. The belief is that con artists frequently use them rather than reveal their residence address. This really isn't true anymore. A great many businesses use post office boxes as their mailing address simply because mail is delivered quicker. We can pick up our mail in the morning from the post office, but have to wait until late afternoon before the mail carrier delivers mail to our office. Because so many businesses use post office boxes nowadays, there is little prejudice against it. In fact, a post office box can make you look more businesslike because you are not using an obvious residence address.

If you don't want to use your residence address and don't want to use a post office box number, you can use a private postal box. These are very popular because you use the street address where the postal box office is located and a suite number to designate your box number. This way it looks like your mailing address is an office rather than a postal box. Postal boxes can be found in most any moderate sized city. Look in the phone book under "Mailing Service" for one in your area. Private postal boxes cost more to rent than post office boxes and, in my opinion, aren't worth it. If you don't plan to move and are relatively stable in your present location, it is probably best to simply use your residence address.

BANK ACCOUNT

If you have chosen a business name other than your own first and last name, you will need to add this name to your bank account. This is so you can deposit checks written out to your business. The bank needs to know that you and your business are the same, and they will need to see the fictitious name statement you obtained at the county courthouse for verification. Some banks may require you to have a business account if you use a fictitious name. This is okay, except they usually charge businesses more processing fees, and minimum balances are usually higher so it costs more for a business account. Some banks will add your business name onto your personal account without problem. You will have to check with your bank and see what their policy is.

STATIONERY

Your next step is to have stationery printed using your business name or your given name, if that is what you are using. Stationery is important because it conveys the image that you are a professional. It is important to present a proper business attitude and appearance. After all, you are approaching clients with a business arrangement so you should conduct yourself properly. Include your business name and mailing address on stationery and envelopes. Also include your phone number. Your client may want to call you to discuss a project and if you do not give your number, he can't easily get ahold of you and may go to someone else.

Along with stationery, you will need manila envelopes, mailers, postage scales, and stamps. Since you will probably be doing most of your work for out of town clients, you will be dealing with the mail. Become familiar with the postage prices. The post office distributes a card which lists postage prices for various weights of letters and packages. Knowing the proper postage and stamping your own mailings will keep you from waiting in often tediously long lines at the post office.

RECORD KEEPING AND TAXES

You will need to keep accurate records of your expenses and income for tax purposes and to regulate the affairs and operation of your business. Record in a ledger all of the expenses you incur in your business. You can deduct expenses up to the amount you earned from your reading services.

What can you deduct? Any expenses related to creating and selling your services. Postage, paper, stationery, typing or other services you use, travel expenses, gasoline usage, phone, etc. Any expense you had to make to do your work is legitimate. If you have an office in your home exclusively set aside for your business, you can deduct the rent or maortgage for that portion of your home. In order to do this, though, the room must be used exclusively for your business and nothing else. For further information on what you can deduct, I highly recommend you go to your local IRS office and pick up their publication *Tax Guide for Small Business* (Publication 334) and *Business Use of Your Home* (Publication 587).You need to do this before you start spending any money in your business so you will be aware of what you can and what you can't deduct, and what will be expected of you when you file your income tax return.

Because you are self-employed, you will not receive W-2 forms from any of the clients you provide services for. W-2 forms are given to employees only. However, businesses may send you a 1099 form, which reports payments made to independent contractors. Like W-2 forms, these payments are reported to the IRS. You may not have deductions taken out of the money you receive, so you need to keep track of how much you earn and how much tax you need to pay. If you earn a substantial amount, your tax obligation could be significant. In order to relieve the burden of paying a large amount of taxes at the end of the year, the IRS requires payment of estimated taxes. These are paid quarterly throughout the tax year. The IRS provides a form 1040ES for this purpose.

Financial record keeping is not only important for tax purposes, but it lets you know how you are doing. You can compare your expenses with your income and see if you are making a profit or just have a time consuming hobby. Keep a file and put all of your receipts in it. You must have proof for each expense you claim as a deduction. If you are ever audited, you will be required to produce these receipts. You will need to keep these records for at least three years. Audits can go back that far. Keep a journal and a file. Write down expenses and payments received. Put all of your receipts in the file. Get receipts for everything, including credit card purchases.

BILLING AND COLLECTIONS

Billing and collections is actually a part of your record keeping. You need to keep a careful record of the invoices you send out and keep track of payments. You can buy standard invoice forms at an office supply store or have personalized invoices with your business name printed. Normal terms for paying on the invoice are net 30 days, which means the client is obligated to pay within 30 days of the date of the invoice. Most businesses who are your clients will pay within 30 days, but some may take 60 or 90. Send late payers a reminder after 30 days and every few weeks thereafter until payment is made. You may simply send a statement as the reminder.

Many businesses charge interest on bills that are not paid on time. In the U.S. a fee of 1.5% per month is currently the maximum you can legally charge. This small amount may not be worth your trouble, but it does serve as a reminder to the client that his bill is increasing the longer he delays payment. As an option, you can offer a five percent discount if payment is made within ten days. This often encourages quick payment. If you have to, you can also pay a collection service to collect for you. If you do this, they will usually take a percentage of the amount owed as their payment. This can amount to 40-50 percent. But even getting a partial payment may be better than nothing.

Most clients pay their bills, but be prepared for the few who don't. For big jobs or for clients that you may feel are questionable, you could ask for half of the payment in advance and the remainder on delivery. Some clients, particularly if no contact is signed, may decide not to follow through with the project after you have completed the work and may not want to pay you for your work. This is a good reason to sign a letter of agreement before starting the project.

WORKING TO SUCCEED

The amount of profit you make and the degree of success you have as a freelance reader will depend largely on the amount of effort you put into your business. You won't have an employer to report to every day, or a boss looking over your shoulder evaluating every move you make. You are responsible only to yourself and your clients. You are free to choose your own work hours and take whatever days off you desire. But if you think working at home is all relaxation and easy work, you need to think twice. Although you do get to stay home and work in an environment that suits your tastes or needs, you will not succeed in any home-based business if you do not devote adequate productive time to your business. Being self-employed requires self-discipline. Your business will only be as successful as you make it. Therefore, you will need to devote adequate time to make it a success. The amount of time and effort you spend and your enthusiasm will determine the degree of success you achieve. Obviously, if you only devote a couple of hours a week to your business, you cannot expect to be bombarded with anxious clients seeking your services. I work with many readers who do a good job and market themselves well. Consequently, these people have more work than they can handle and are forced to turn down many jobs. They are happy and successful in their careers. Other readers who are not so ambitious or skilled have more spare time than they would probably like. The amount of work you receive depends on the amount of effort you put into your business.

Besides spending time, you will need to spend some money. It is a general rule that making money requires spending money. Home-based businesses are no different. Some home-based businesses require a substantial outlay of capital, while others require almost none. Fortunately, a reading service can be set up with a minimal amount of investment. Since you work out of your home, your overhead expenses are minor. Your initial expenses will be the purchase of stationery and ledgers for record keeping. A wordprocessor or computer is a necessary tool for most readers. If you don't have this type of equipment you will need to consider it. Your biggest expense will probably be in marketing your services. This will include the cost of producing flyers, sales letters, and brochures, as well as postage, telephone expenses, and the like. Advertising, in other words, will take the biggest bite out of your expenses. But advertising is necessary in order to get clients and is another key aspect of your success. Advertising and marketing your services are discussed more fully in the next chapter.

Books I highly recommend for helping you set up and run a successful home-based business are *Homemade Money* and *Help for Your Growing Homebased Business,* both by Barbara

Brabec, and *Small-Time Operator* by Bernard Kamoroff. Another excellent resource is the *National Home Business Report*. This is a newsletter written specifically for people who operate home-based businesses. It discusses the problems and challenges home workers face, and provides solutions and networking opportunities. For further information, write to the *National Home Business Report*, Dept. CO-10, P.O. Box 2137, Naperville, IL 60567. A couple of other newsletters aimed at home-based businesses are *Home Office Opportunities*, P.O. Box 780, Lyman, WY 82937 and *Your Successful Home Office*, P.O. Box 244, Dillon Beach, CA 94929.

CHAPTER 4

MARKETING YOUR SERVICES

As a freelance reader you will be self-employed, so you must find clients who need your services. Some will use your services repeatedly, while others will need you only once. You will likely need to be continually seeking new clients in order to earn a steady income. As you saw in Chapter 2, almost any type of business and many individuals can use readers, so there is a huge market available to you. In this chapter, you will learn how to approach new clients and get their business.

Many large companies have employees who research, edit, and proofread much of the material they produce. Small businesses usually do not. They create their own material and have someone in the office proofread it. Although large companies are potential clients, the small business owner is in greater need of your services. Any type of business could use your services. Look in the phone book for possible businesses to approach. Look particularly for businesses that do a lot of advertising, such as car dealers, lawyers, health spas, etc. Some businesses lend themselves particularly well to the services of readers because they work with customers who are involved in printing, publishing, or writing. Some examples would be publishers, print shops, typesetting services, graphic designers, advertising agencies, public relations firms, and the like.

The need for competent readers is there. Often, many people and businesses who need your services don't even realize it, and all it takes is a little convincing. Let your services be known, tell potential clients what you can do for them, and customers will come. I am a firm believer in using editors and proofreaders for any material that will be published or is meant to be read by other people. I've learned from experience that mistakes are easy to make, yet often difficult to spot yourself, and another person is beneficial in weeding out those errors that seem to slip by unnoticed.

HOW TO FIND CLIENTS

There are several ways you can approach potential clients. You can use phone solicitation, personal contacts, published advertisements, or send information describing your services through the mail. If you have the ability to talk convincingly with people and are not timid, you can contact potential clients personally or by phone. Most people, however, do not feel comfortable with this direct approach. This tactic also restricts you to your local area. By using advertisements and mailings, your client potential is greatly enhanced, and you are not required to verbally manipulate a customer into using your services. You can also reach thousands of more people in much less time. Unless you are a natural born salesman, I suggest you concentrate on using ads and mailings to publicize your services.

You must build and maintain a list of prospective clients. You will have some satisfied clients who will continue to use your services for many years. Many others will only need you for a single project. If you plan on making a decent part-time income or earn a living as a reader, you will need to continually seek new clients.

Publishers and writers usually know the importance of readers, but the average aspiring writer or businessman may not.

Most businesses will be a little more reluctant to hire you because not only must you sell yourself and your skills, but you must also sell these companies on the importance of your services. When contacting businesses, if possible, use the name of the person responsible for the type of service you offer. You can find this information by phoning the company and asking the receptionist. Don't bother to explain what you are doing, simply ask for the name of the person in charge of advertising or sales promotion or whoever is most likely to use your services.

There are several ways to get contacts. The best is through recommendations from satisfied customers. Other ways which will build your clientele list are classified advertising and direct mail promotion, each of which is discussed below.

CHEAP ADVERTISING AND PUBLICITY

The least expensive way to let people know of your services is by word of mouth advertising. Satisfied customers will tell their friends and business associates about you and bring additional business. I recommend that you have some business cards printed up so you can pass them out to all your customers. The business card not only provides clients information on how to contact you, but also serves as a reminder that you are available. You can get 500 to 1000 cards printed for about $30. They are well worth the cost. Give your cards out freely to anyone you meet who you think might use your services. You can visit businesses that have bulletin boards and put your business card up. Such boards are frequently found in laudromats, grocery stores, churches, and other places. You can also visit some appropriate businesses that might be willing to display your card—such as print shops and art supply stores.

Put your business cards or flyers up at college campuses. You may need to check with the administration office before you do this, as some colleges have restrictions on what and where material like this can be displayed. You can also pass out flyers or put them on windshields. At colleges, everyone is a potential client, teachers and students alike, so you can approach them all.

CLASSIFIED ADS

Classified ads are the cheapest type of paid advertising. You are usually charged so much per word. This figure can vary from a few cents to several dollars per word depending on the publication.

You can advertise in newspapers or magazines. If you are interested in the local market, you can use the newspaper or a local magazine. However, you can get a better response by selecting appropriate national magazines—magazines whose readership are composed of the type of people who would most likely use your services. Some magazines would be those aimed at publishers, writers, and students. Student newspapers would be a good source. Trade magazines for publishers and writers would be another excellent source. Refer to *Writer's Market* for appropriate magazines.

Once you have a list of magazines, write to the advertising department and ask for classified advertising rates and deadline dates. You will receive material providing you with the prices and dates for several months or a full year. You will also note that most of the larger magazines require your ad be sent in about two months before publication.

Some of these magazines even have subheadings in the classified section for editors, indexers, critiquing services, etc. Look at the ads in writers' magazines for examples of classified ads. Model you ad on those which most impress you. Keep your ad brief and to the point.

Typically, the cost for classified advertising will run $4-$8 per word. This includes your address, phone number, zip code—everything. Once you start writing the ad, you will discover it is quite easy to say too much and end up with an ad that costs $300 or more. With a little rewriting and editing, you can trim down your ad to the bare bones. Say just enough to get your message across, but no more than necessary to keep expenses down.

In the ad below there are 37 words. Assuming $5 a word, it would cost $185 to run this ad.

> Manuscript editing and critiquing services. Don't trust your writing to just anyone. Published editor will edit or critique your manuscript at reasonable rates. Fast, reliable service. Contact Joe Wilson, Easy Edit, 639 Upton Avenue, Sacramento, CA 95825.

The following ad says basically the same thing as the one above, with only 12 words for a cost of only $60.

> Editing, critiquing. Fast reliable service. Easy Edit, 639 Upton, Sacramento, CA 95825.

When advertising editing or literary services with trade magazines for writers such as *Writer's Digest*, you will be required to submit a resume and a sample of your work. These magazines require samples in an effort to ensure that all advertisers are competent and legitimate. This requirement isn't a guarantee on the advertiser's performance, but it cuts out some who should not offer such services.

DIRECT MAIL

You may also approach potential clients through direct mail. Send information on your services to a select group of people who are most likely to use your services. If, for example, you have a degree in law and are interested in technical reading or editing of legal material, you can send advertising literature to lawyers. If you want to contact writers, publishers, or business owners, you can get a mailing list of these people.

There are many mailing list companies who collect and sell lists. Prices range from about $10 per thousand names to $90 per thousand, with the typical price being in the $60-$80 range. Some mailing list companies require a minimum order of two to five thousand names. The names usually come on mailing labels, either Cheshire (ungummed) or pressure sensitive (pregummed). The Cheshire labels require a special gumming machine to stick them onto the envelopes, so your best bet is to get the pressure sensitive labels which you peel and stick.

When you buy a list of names, what you are really buying are the labels themselves and not the names on the labels. In reality, you are only renting the names and can use them only one time. That means you cannot copy the names down and send additional mailings to the same list. In order to reuse the names, you must rent the list again and make another payment.

You may be thinking, how would the list company know if you use the names again? The lists are seeded with dummy names which go back to the list company. If they get an unauthorized mailing, they will bill you again for the use of the list.

Another way to get mailing lists is to contact magazines and rent a list of their subscribers. Be selective. Don't use any list. Use a list of specific types of people who will be likely to use your services. A list of auto mechanics will not be as receptive as a list of writers, for instance. Choose wisely. In the appendix I have included several reputable mailing list companies who offer lists of names of hundreds of different professions, businesses, and organizations.

There are many directories you can find in your local library with lists of business, organization, and association names. I've mentioned *Literary Market Place* and *Writer's Market*. These directories list the major publishing companies, but many smaller companies that would be prime prospects for your services are not listed. You can find them, as well as other businesses that would be receptive to your services, in the phone book. Most libraries have phone book collections covering many different cities throughout the country. You can do a little research and create your own list of publishers, print shops, advertising agencies, etc. to contact.

If you send a minimum of 200 letters, you can send them by bulk rate mail, which costs about a third less than first class mail. When you're sending out several hundred letters this cost savings can be significant. But in order to qualify to send bulk mailings, you must register with the post office and pay an annual fee for a bulk mail permit. If your mailings will be small and you plan on using the permit only once or twice, it may not be worth your time and expense. However, if you want to contact several hundred or thousand potential clients, bulk mail is one of the cheapest ways to do it. Contact your local post office. They will be more than happy to answer your questions about bulk mailings and will give you a booklet describing this service in detail.

SALES PACKAGE

Whether you approach a prospective client in person, by direct mail, or by classified advertising, you will need to give him some material describing your services and qualifications. This material will be some combination of the following: cover letter, resume, brochure, and supporting information (i.e., endorsements, clips, work samples). This material will be the vehicle you use to convince clients to use your services and will also serve as a reminder to him that you are available.

We keep a file of the readers we use. Having this information helps us choose an appropriate person for any particular job. When we need editing, proofreading, or indexing, we go to our file and choose an appropriate person to do it.

One of the things that strongly suggests to me that a potential reader is a competent professional is the type and quality of the material he or she sends to me. A cover letter introducing you and offering your services is a must. Don't just send a resume or business card. The resume gives your credentials and describes your background, training, schooling, and work experience—all important to a potential client's evaluation of your ability. You can also include a flyer or short brochure describing your services. In some cases, this can replace both the cover letter and resume. Anyone who is professional enough to have flyers produced is serious about their work. Producing flyers costs money, so you show confidence in yourself.

Send all prospective clients your sales package. If you do not get an immediate response from a prospective client, don't take it as a rejection of your offer. On the contrary, the client may be very interested in your services but not have a project for you at the time. He may file your inquiry for later reference. We file all information from freelancers which we might possibly use. When the need arises, we look through our files for an appropriate person to do the job. You might continue to send information occasionally, just to remind both new and old clients you are still available. Many clients don't realize, at first, how much they need your services and may pass over your first letter. After the idea of using readers has had time to sink in, a client may be hooked by second letter.

Cover Letter

Remember you are approaching a prospective client with a business proposition. As such, you need to present yourself in a businesslike manner. Use stationery with your imprinted letter-head. Do not send a hand written letter; be professional. Type the letter in a proper business format. No "To Whom It May Concern" stuff. Address your letter to a specific person, if possible. If you can't get a name, use a title such as "Managing Editor" or "Advertising Manager"

The purpose of the letter is to introduce you and your service to the prospective client. It should not be a life history or filled with descriptions of the books you have read. Get straight to the point and limit your pitch to one page. Proclaiming that you have a love for reading, or the fact that you read ten novels a week just for fun, serves no worthwhile purpose. The fact that you are seeking this type of job already indicates your interest in reading, and just because you read a lot does not qualify you to be a good reader. Simply tell the prospective client who you are and what you have to offer. People are busy and will spend only a few seconds reading sales letters, so you need to get your message across quickly. The details or nitty gritty can be stated elsewhere in your mailing. If prospective clients are interested they will read more. Don't try to be too cute or you may lose the reader. You can start with an interesting or provocative statement

EXAMPLE 1

DAVID JONES INDEXING
P.O. BOX 8522
ROSEVILLE, CA 95678
916/543-5847

May 5, 19--

James G. Smith
McGill Press
654 Broadway
New York, NY 10021

Dear Mr. Smith:
I am sending you this letter to offer my
services as an indexer. I can index books on a broad
range of subjects. I am particularly experienced in
the areas of business and finance, real estate,
personal financial planning, and communications.
I have been a freelance indexer for two years
and have a thorough knowledge and intuitive sense of
the field. I received training as an indexer with
Westside Press in San Rafael, California, where I
worked as an editorial assistant for four years. I
have been an active member of The American Society
of Indexers for the past three years.
Please consider my services the next time you
need an index. If you have any questions or would
just like to get acquainted, please feel free to give
me a call.

Sincerely,

David Jones

Sample cover letters set in a an acceptable business format are illustrated on pages 41, 42, and 43.

EXAMPLE 2

```
        WORDS RIGHT EDITORIAL SERVICE
              23 MAIN STREET
            SACRAMENTO, CA 95834
               916/756-9675
```

May 5, 19--

James G. Smith
McGill Press
654 Broadway
New York, NY 10021

Dear Mr. Smith:
    I am a freelance editor and would like to offer my services to you.
    I've been editing for three years and for the past two years have operated my own full-time freelance editing service. I can guarantee you fast, dependable service. Some of my past clients include Doubleday Books, Addison-Wesley Publishing Co., Bucknell Press, Firebrand Books, Longman Publishing Group, Peachtree Publishers, and Regal Books.
    Enclosed you will find a copy of my resume and a recent article published by <u>Redbook</u> that I edited for author Susan Strawberry. I have also had several of my own articles published in various magazines, including <u>Better Homes and Gardens</u>, <u>Texas Monthly</u>, and <u>Southern Living.</u>
    Please give me a call the next time your company is looking for an editor. I look forward to hearing from you in the near future. Thank you for your attention to my inquiry.

Sincerely,

Brenda Hill

EXAMPLE 3

ROSS RESEARCH
384 SEVENTH STREET
LINCOLN, NE 68506
402/978-2630

May 5, 19--

James G. Smith
McGill Press
654 Broadway
New York, NY 10021

Dear Mr. Smith:

I would like to offer my services to you as a researcher. I have a bachelor's degree in library science and have had 16 years experience working in the Los Angeles Public Library, one of the largest and most complete libraries in the country. For the past seven years I have also operated my own research service. My knowledge of the library system and reference materials has been the focus of my success.

Some of my clients include the Easter Seal Foundation, The Rochester Health Clinic, Pepsi-Cola Corporation, California Publishers Association, Unicorp, and IBM, to mention just a few.

My resume is enclosed for your reference. I have also included a letter of recommendation from William Stands, director of the Los Angeles Public Library and chairman of the Library Board in Los Angeles County.

Please keep my materials on file for any jobs that become available and notify me if you need other information. Thank you for your time.

Sincerely,

Terri Ross

or opening sentence to grab their interest, but come quickly to the point.

If you do not have a printed letterhead on your stationery, you can center and type across the top your name, address, and phone number. Although this is acceptable, printed stationery is more impressive.

Don't lie about your abilities or qualifications—it will be obvious in your writing. Also, go over your letter very carefully, checking for errors. Your cover letter serves as a sample of your literary skill. If your are trying to sell your literary services and your letter is filled with spelling and grammatical errors, no client will hire you. After all, if that is the service you are offering and you can't compose an error free letter for yourself, how can anyone trust you with their material?

Resume

After the cover letter, the resume would be next in importance in your sales package. You may include brief personal information, but more important, include details and dates on schooling, work experience, publishing credits, special awards or honors, and business references.

Resumes come in many different formats and styles. Use the same type you would give to a prospective employer. See the following two-page example. This resume provides needed information for the client to judge your qualifications.

Endorsements

Comments and endorsements from satisfied customers are a big advantage to you. Anybody can make claims about themselves, but favorable comments from clients verify your competence.

Many clients will write favorable comments to you if you've done a good job. You can use these quotations in any promotional literature you use. Also, you may solicit comments from repeat or satisfied customers. Obviously, if a client uses your services more than once, he was satisfied with your work. You must, however, have written permission to use any private quotation. If you do not get written approval you could offend a valuable customer. If you want to use comments from customers,

RESUME

Patricia Elliott
94 Parkway Road
Fountain, CO 80817
(719) 295-8743

PROFESSIONAL EXPERIENCE

3/91-Present   **Freelance Editor and Proofreader**
Patricia Elliott Editing Services, Fountain, CO

4/88 - 3/91   **Assistant Editor**
Daily Gazette, Lodi, CA
Wrote weekly column "Uptown" and reported on community events.

5/87 - 3/88   **Literary Specialist**
Wilderness Foundation, Fort Collins, CO
Proofread and edited foundation newsletter and publicity materials.

8/85 - 5/87   **Teaching Assistant**
New York University, New York City, NY
Taught undergraduate English classes.

9/83 - 8/85   **Assistant Manager**
The Book Worm, New York City, NY
Floor manager of general interest bookstore responsible for sales, special promotions, and publicity.

EDUCATION

B.A. in English, May 1985, GPA: 3.48/4.00, New York University, New York City, New York
M.A. in Journalism, May 1987, GPA: 3.60/4.00, New York University, New York City, New York

COLLEGE ACTIVITIES

Sigma Tau Delta, English Honors Society
Caesura, Assistant Editor

HONORS

Julian Pierce Excellence in Journalism Award,1990
San Luis Obispo Literary Guild's First Person Award,1989
National Association of Journalists Outstanding Student Achievement, 1988
1st Place New York University Thinking Essay Contest, 1985

PROFESSIONAL ASSOCIATIONS

Editorial Freelancers Association
Colorado Editors Association

REFERENCES

Excellent personal and professional references are available and will be furnished upon request.

ask for written permission first. A brief letter of approval with a signature is sufficient.

Clips and Writing Credits

If you have had any of your own writing published, either as a book or magazine article, let the client know. These publishing credits demonstrate your literary skill. They are particularly helpful for literary critics, book reviewers, manuscript readers, technical readers, editors, and proofreaders, but can be beneficial to all types of readers. It is difficult to get published and if you have accomplished this feat, you demonstrate to your potential client that you have proven skills.

If appropriate, you can even send copies or clips of the article or portions of a published book of yours. Write on the clip the name of the publisher or publication and the date of publication. The more prestigious the publisher or publication, the more impressive. Obviously, if you had an article published in *Cosmopolitan*, it would be much more impressive than one from the *Brewery Digest*. Publishing credits from small magazines are valuable, just not as impressive as those from popular consumer magazines.

Do not use small local community or church newsletters as proof of your literary ability as these types of publications do not necessarily indicate any particular skill in writing. The fact that you even mention such an article indicates you are straining for credibility. If, however, you are the editor of a newsletter, mention the fact. This indicates that you probably do have some marketable skills.

If you don't have any publishing credits, don't say anything about it, and don't say you have written a book or article but haven't found a publisher yet. These are negative statements. Only mention the positive—material that has actually been printed.

Since being a published author gives you credibility, you may want to try to get magazine articles published. I have included an entire chapter (Chapter 6) on how to get articles published in magazines so you can have publishing credits. In that chapter I explain which publications are the easiest to get published in. Many magazines which will provide you with good, useable publishing credits are actually very receptive to new authors, and it is surprisingly easy to get an article published in them. I will show you how.

Brochures

You may also include a flyer or brochure. This can be a single sheet of paper for a flyer or a single sheet folded into a small brochure. The flyer or brochure need not be large, an 8½ x 11-inch size paper folded twice will do the job. You usually won't need more space than this. Keep the sales pitch short and simple for best results.

You may include a picture of yourself. Visual impact has proven to be effective in sales literature. Include endorsements and favorable comments from past clients. List qualifications, achievements, special awards, experience, and writing credits. Describe your services. Give your name, address, and phone number. A physical address is preferred over a post office box. A street address allows your clients to send material by UPS or Federal Express, which cannot easily be delivered to a post office box.

You can use the flyer or brochure in place of the resume, and possibly even the cover letter, since they contain basically the same information.

A professional looking flyer will indicate a professional attitude and quality service.

Show Your Skill

All new readers, particularly editors and proofreaders, are looked upon with some degree of apprehension by new clients and by publishers in particular. Many publishers are flooded with requests from potential "readers," most of which have no knowledge what the publisher's needs are, nor possess adequate skill to properly edit, proofread, or evaluate their material. This situation has arisen thanks to con artists who have sold people on the idea they can be paid for reviewing manuscripts.

Because so many unqualified people are attempting to be "readers" or editors and proofreaders, you need to show your potential clients that you have the qualifications and skills to do a good job. There are of couple of ways you can do this.

The simplest way to show your skill is to include with your sales package a short sample of your editing. Keep it brief, no more than two or three pages. Use a portion of a manuscript or a short article or report. You could choose an actual assignment you have worked on, or create a report yourself to edit. If you use material from another client, you must get his permission before doing so. If you create your own article or report, you have full control over the use and presentation of the material. Or you could have a friend write an essay which you edit.

Another way to demonstrate your skill is to offer to do the first project for free. This way the client can test your skills without obligation. Possibly limit the page length so you don't get an epic novel of 500 pages. Clients are impressed by such an offer because it demonstrates your willingness to prove your ability and that you have confidence in yourself. Many clients will be impressed just because you made the offer and will assign you a project without a test. I believe an offer like this is the best thing you can do to win new clients who will eventually become repeat customers. Obviously, customers who may only use your services once or twice would not warrant receiving an offer like this, so be selective. Publishers and writers would be good candidates for this type of offer, students would not.

Most editors and proofreaders who contact us do not offer to demonstrate their skills as described above. Since we do not know the abilities of new readers, frequently we will test them with a short assignment. I have found a vast difference in skill and competence level. Some editors simply give a review or opinion of the material without changing or correcting the text much; others do detailed editing and include many good comments and suggestions for improvement. Responses like the first are totally worthless and they are never given any further assignments. We look for editors and proofreaders who will do the best and most complete job.

Additional information about marketing your services can be obtained from the sources listed in the appendix.

CHAPTER 5

GUIDELINES FOR SUCCESS

In this chapter I will discuss some topics which will help to make your business a success.

ACCURACY

I cannot stress enough the importance of doing a good job. If you do a poor or inadequate job, you won't get repeat business. Once you are established and have proven yourself to clients, a large percentage of your business will come from your current list of clients. Therefore, it is important that you do a good job. There is no faking this type of work, especially if you work for a publisher or writer who is familiar with working with readers. They will spot your errors or mistakes.

In regard to copy editors and proofreaders, it is almost impossible for any one editor to catch every single mistake in a good-sized manuscript. There has never been a book published that did not contain some errors when it was first published (even this book undoubtedly contains some minor errors), but editing is supposed to eliminate at least 99.99 percent of them. If multiple errors are still found in a manuscript after you have edited it, you will lose a client or not be paid.

Read the material twice. This is particularly true for editors and proofreaders. It is amazing how many errors you will miss if you only read a text once. Always read at least twice. Many times, reading the material a second time will make parts of the text clearer and problems that were skipped on the first reading can be properly addressed.

I have worked with new editors who have not done acceptable jobs. While looking over corrections they made in our manuscripts, I've found dozens of mistakes they missed. I turn around and send the material back and have them redo it until the editing is acceptable. Obviously, if I have to do something this drastic, I am not likely to use that person again. Bad experiences have caused us to be very cautious and selective of who we use. And because we have so many editors on file, we can be very selective.

DEADLINES

Be very conscious of time. Some businesses, publishers in particular, work around a tight time schedule with strict deadlines. You will therefore have to complete the work when requested. This is also true for term papers and theses from students who must hand in their reports by a designated time. There is no excuse for being late! As a publisher, I cannot work with any reader who cannot meet my time restraints.

If you live in the same city as your client, you can personally deliver the manuscript. However, if you live or work some distance away, you will need to mail it. In this case you must allow adequate time for delivery! If the client says he needs the material by the 10th of the month, don't put it in the mail on the 9th. Mail service is very inconsistent. I have received mail from across the country within two days, but I have also had to wait ten days to receive mail sent from only 40 miles away.

If time is of no concern, you can send manuscripts through the U.S. mail fourth class. This will save you about two dollars in postage over first class priority mail, but will require as much as two or three weeks for delivery. However, most clients want their materials back as soon as possible. Therefore, you should send it second day priority mail. The postal service doesn't guarantee delivery in two days, but they will usually come close. So, allow at least three days for delivery by priority mail.

To be on the safe side you can send the manuscript by Express Mail, Federal Express, UPS next day air, or some similar service. These services guarantee delivery in one day. They are several times more expensive than priority mail, but at least your delivery is guaranteed. You might also consider a second day service, such as that offered by UPS (blue label, second day service). They will guarantee delivery within two days for about half the price of overnight delivery. This is still more expensive than priority mail, but significantly less expensive than any overnight delivery service.

If no deadline is mentioned, don't take it to mean there isn't one and take your time. Call to confirm a time, or complete the work in a timely manner. Short jobs may be completed within one or two days. Larger jobs may take a couple of weeks or more. Do the job as quickly as possible.

There is no acceptable excuse for delivering a manuscript late! None! Deadlines must be met, regardless of any emergencies or problems you may encounter. Your clients are depending on you to do the work and return their material on time. Any delay, regardless of the excuse, will kill your chances of working with that client on future projects. If you do have a problem that would delay your work, let the client know at once and return the material if necessary. This way, he can either allow you some extra time or assign the work to someone else and still meet his deadline.

I had one new reader to whom I sent a small 40-page manuscript, requesting a turnaround time of a week. When it didn't arrive, I tried to contact her. I couldn't reach her by phone, so I wrote to her. She wrote back to apologize, stating that the delay was because she was in the process of moving and didn't have time to get to the manuscript, but would do so soon. It eventually took her over five weeks. Needless to say I would never consider using her again, no matter how good a job she could do. Keep in mind that even one day late can be a costly delay for the client.

RATES

The rates readers are paid varies widely depending on the type and size of the job, the financial position of the company, and your experience. Book and periodical publishers usually set their own rates and pay somewhat less than other businesses. People and businesses outside of the publishing industry will expect you to have a fee schedule. Most readers can average around $10 to $25 an hour or more. If you have special training and are experienced, you could earn as much as $60 an hour.

Be competitive. If your rates are too high, clients will find others to do the job or simply have their secretary do it essentially for nothing. If you are a new reader and relatively inexperienced, you might charge less for your services than someone who has had several years of experience. You may also charge less initially in order to work with a client who may bring you substantial repeat business.

I prefer to pay freelance editors by the page because that way, I can determine the exact cost before the project begins and plan for it in our budget. It is also generally the easiest way for the reader to keep track of and bill for payment. When you do copyediting by the page, it should be understood that a page is considered typed and double-spaced with 1 to $1^{1}/_{4}$-inch margins on every side. Writers and publishers understand this because that is how all manuscripts should be formatted. Since material from other clients may vary in format, an hourly scale may be better for you.

If you base your fee on an hourly scale, clients will usually request an estimate on the length of time for each assignment. If you are a proofreader, you can estimate this relatively easily because you should know about how many pages you can cover in an hour. For editors and other types of readers, your time will depend on the text. Some texts are more difficult than others because of the audience they are written for. A teenage novel, for example, would be much easier to read than an in-depth guide to real estate investing or financial planning. Also, some texts may be very well-written and require very little editing, while others may require massive corrections to the point of almost rewriting the text. You may want to spend some time working on the manuscript to get a feel for the job and thereby give an accurate estimate of the time that will be involved.

If the job turns out to be more difficult than originally expected, you may go back and renegotiate the fee with the client. Price changes should be kept to a minimum because clients do not like having to readjust their expenses. You may consider a set fee per hour or page that will be an average and stick close to it. Some projects will take a little longer than others, but on the average things even out without the hassle of renegotiating the fee and, therefore, you maintain a good relationship with your clients. A reader who frequently changes his fees during a project will lose customers.

You should consider having a letter of agreement signed by both parties, indicating the work to be done and the fee to be paid. You could include in the letter that you are estimating the time and that your fee is based on a certain number of hours. If more time is required, you have the right to renegotiate with the client.

If you charge by the hour, you must keep accurate track of your time. Since you will start and stop at different times throughout the day, keeping accurate tabs on your time can get difficult if you do not use a system of some sort. Keep a ledger and write down every time you start and finish, including breaks. Calculate the total number of hours spent at the end of each day. Besides the time you actually spend on the project itself, you may also include time you spend on the phone with or typing correspondence to the client, since that is all part of the job. Include research time, time delivering material to the post office, printing and copying, and any time necessary to complete and deliver the job.

Once the job is complete, send in the material with your invoice. What should you charge? Below is a listing of fees which are currently being charged by professional readers. This data was compiled from information printed in *Writer's Market*, from my own personal experience, and from working readers.

Article reading/clipping: Up to $300 per article.

Book manuscript reading, nonspecialized subjects: $20-$50 for a summary and recommendation. **Specialized subjects:** $250-$500 and up, depending on the project. For a book club or film producer: $50-$100 per book.

Book reviews: Byline and copy of the reviewed book for small newspapers; $35-$300 for larger publications.

Clipping service reading: $5-$12 and up per hour.

Critique article manuscript: $30-60 per article or short story up to 3,000 words.

Critique book manuscript: $160 for outline and first 20,000 words; $300-$500 for up to 100,000 words.

Editing: $7-$50 per hour; $1-$5 per page; $100-$5,000 per manuscript, based on size and complexity of the project.

Indexing: $8-$22 per hour; $1-$6 per page; or flat fee of $200-$500 depending on length.

Literary agent: 10-20 percent commission plus fees.

Proofreading: $6-$12 per hour and up; $0.50-$3 per page.

Research: $10-$40 and up per hour; flat fee of $200-$500, depending on complexity.

Student reading: $6-$8 per hour.

Technical editing: $15-$60 per hour.

Technical proofreading: $10-$30 per hour.

Translation, commercial: $100-$120 for common European languages. More for other languages. **Government agencies:** $20-$120 per 1,000 foreign words into English. **Literary:** $40-$100 per thousand English words. **Technical:** $125 per thousand words.

Rates for all reading services vary, and change with supply and demand. If you want a current estimate of the going rates, inquire with people who are doing it. Look in the classified ad section of publications such as *Writer's Digest* and find proofreaders, literary critics, indexers, researchers, translators, and the like. Write to them as if you were a potential client and ask how much they charge. You will also get a good sampling of the types of advertising literature they send out. Some of it will be very simple or even amateurish, and some will be very professional. The professionally done material will have a more accurate fix on the current prices being charged by working professionals.

EDUCATION AND TRAINING

Of all of the types of readers discussed in this book, the only ones who need a college education or some type of formal training are technical readers/editors and copy editors. Although not absolutely necessary, a college degree is also advised for translators. Translators can learn their craft by experience and personal study, but they must pass a test to be certified by the American Translators Association. A college education is beneficial for several types of readers and provides credentials verifying skill. Clients will look at your formal training when considering using your services. If they are going to pay for a service, they want to make sure it will be done competently. You should have the skills to do a good job.

Reading service skills can be learned or refined as part of a regular job working for somebody else. However, most of these skills can be learned simply by personal study and experience. Taking a few select college courses can greatly enhance your knowledge and understanding, and is highly recommended. Classes in library science, English, and creative writing being the most beneficial.

Another aspect potential clients look at is the length of time you have been involved in this type of work, either with another company or as a freelancer. Being self-employed for several years as a freelance reader is a sign of success and competence. The best type of training for most readers is simply experience.

Experience can make up for a lack of formal education. Traditionally, most reading jobs have been performed by writers. Although you don't need to be a writer to be a good reader, it helps to have some writing competency. Student readers, clipping service readers, indexers, researchers, and the like don't need a great deal of creative writing background. But all readers can benefit from having good writing skills. Having had some of your writing published in a magazine or book shows clients you have these skills, and for copy editors, book reviewers, literary critics, agents, and others, publication is a strong endorsement. I recommend readers sharpen their writing skills and get something published (see Chapter 6).

Another way to gain experience and improve your skills is by belonging to an appropriate association or club. Membership in these organizations shows clients you are a professional and seriously involved in your career. There are many benefits of being a member of such groups. They provide classes, seminars, training materials, newsletters, reports, and group support. They keep you in touch with new developments and trends in the profession, and allow you to have personal contact with others who are doing the same thing as you are. Personal contact gives you the opportunity to network with other working professionals. You can exchange ideas, experiences, concerns, solve problems, and gain insight on improving your skills and marketing your services better.

The key to success for any service related business is to do a good job. Make your customers happy. Although many of your clients will only need your services once, if you do a good job some customers will continue to work with you. Publishing companies can provide you regular assignments almost indefinitely if you do a good job for them. Writers and other individuals likewise will continue to work with you. It is much easier and cheaper to get repeat business from former clients than it is to seek out new customers. Also, if your clients are pleased with your services, they will recommend you to others and your business will grow. If you are to succeed as a freelance reader, do the best job you can for each client and continue to better yourself by taking advantage of any available classes or training.

CHAPTER 6

HOW TO BECOME A PUBLISHED AUTHOR

If you are interested in becoming a freelance reader, you no doubt have a love for literature and have probably entertained the thought of becoming a published author yourself. Perhaps you have even tried to get some of your own writing published and, like most people, discovered it is not an easy task.

In this chapter I will explain the quickest and easiest way of getting published and earning valuable writing credits. It is not as hard as you might think. In fact, it is rather simple if you know how to go about it. *If you have average writing skills, you can get published!*

If you have had a book or magazine article published, you have a valuable writing credit that could help open up doors of opportunity to you. Although writing skill or being published is by no means a requirement to becoming a reader, it can enhance your chances with some reading jobs. This is particularly true for manuscript readers, book reviewers, technical readers, copy editors, proofreaders, literary critics, and literary agents. Listing books or articles that you have had published on your resume shows you have some degree of literary competence. I would highly recommend any of the above listed readers obtain as many writing credits as possible. It is for this reason that I have included this chapter. In fact, you may find the joy of having your works published and getting paid for it are very rewarding, and you may want to devote your time to pursuing a writing career. I will focus my discussion on getting published in magazines. Book publishing is much more involved and much more difficult. Although, if you have ever tried to get an article published, you may believe it to be just as difficult, and it is if you don't know how to go about it. Trying to get published in the popular consumer magazines is no easier than trying to get a book published. There are, however, many credible publications that are very receptive to authors of all skill levels, and you can get articles published in them relatively easily. This is where you can start building your writing credits. Even popular consumer magazine and book publishers will look more favorably on you if you have writing credits, thus increasing your chances of getting published with them.

There are thousands of periodicals, ranging from the purely scientific to association newsletters to general interest magazines. The degree of writing skill required by them varies. Some publications are very selective and may consider rejecting a manuscript if a single grammar or spelling error is found. On the other hand, there are many small publications which welcome almost any relevant topic regardless of the author's literary skill. The popular newsstand magazines are very selective and consequently pay the best. Lesser known publications, however, pay very little or nothing at all. The big advantage of having an article published by these smaller publications is that it provides you with experience and writing credits. Although having been published in popular well known magazines is most impressive, writing credits from lesser known publications are valuable too. You can develop good writing skills and writing credits by writing for small publications.

As a publisher, I am much more impressed with a person who has had several articles published by a small magazine than someone who has had nothing published at all. I also like receiving sample articles or clips from potential readers I work with because it proves they have writing experience and shows they have confidence in their work. Send no more than three clips. You do not need to overwhelm the client with your writing credits. Send the complete article and write the name of the publisher and publication date on the piece.

THE ARTICLES MARKET

Consumer and Trade Publications

There are two major types of periodicals: consumer magazines and trade publications. Consumer magazines are purchased in newsstands or by subscription. They can be general interest publications such as *Reader's Digest* and *Life,* or slanted toward a special interest such as *Sports Afield, Seventeen,* and *Mature Living.* Articles in these publications are meant to inform and entertain. The trade journal or newsletter, on the other hand, is a voice of an industry or an association. Information contained in them has to be detailed and specific.

Writer's Market contains an extensive listing of consumer and trade publications. A sample of some of the publications listed include *The Lawyer's Word, Coal People Magazine, Golf Shop Operations, Print & Graphics, Juggler's World,* and *Pet Age.* However, *Writer's Market* only lists publications which are actively looking for freelance submissions. There are thousands of smaller publications which are not listed. Many associations and other organizations publish magazines and newsletters and welcome freelance submissions, although they frequently do not offer the author payment, except perhaps in the form of a few copies of the publication. These are still legitimate publications that will provide good writing experience and credit. No matter what your interests are, you are bound to find publications devoted to them. So how do you track down these publications? A list of associations and newsletters is given in several sources listed in the appendix.

Small Publications

New writers often make the mistake of trying to sell only to the largest and most popular magazines. These magazines receive literally thousands of submissions every month, but buy only a very few. Your chances of breaking into print with one of these giants are extremely small. *Redbook*, for example, receives 3,000 short story submissions every month but publishes only two or three of them in each issue. Your chances of selling a manuscript to them is one in 1,000! Obviously, not very good odds. However, if you go to a much smaller publication such as *Flipside*, which receives five to six submissions a month and publishes six to eight a year, your chances increase to one in ten. For this reason alone it is generally much easier to get into print with the smaller publications.

Many of the smaller publications are hungry for material and will accept almost any article for publication that is targeted toward the publication's readership. Any budding writer should be able to get published somewhere. Getting published in these small publications is a stepping-stone. As you gain more experience and your writing skills improve, you can approach the more prestigious publications with a greater probability of success.

Payment for articles varies widely from publication to publication. The popular consumer magazines with large circulations will pay anywhere from $1,000 to $5,000 for feature articles. This is a major reason why they are swamped with submissions and why competition is so fierce. More typically you can expect payment of around $200 or $300 from most modest sized publications.

Some of the smaller publications and technical journals frequently pay with a free subscription or a few sample copies of the issue which contains your article. Many small publications don't offer anything other than to include your byline, and you may even have to purchase the issue to get a copy of your printed article. This doesn't mean these publications are not respected or that getting published in them is worthless—it's not. You will gain experience and a publishing credit you can use as a reference in future sales literature.

Admittedly, it is more impressive to an editor if you have been published in a major consumer magazine, but for a beginner it is almost impossible. Start with the smaller publications and work your way up. Don't try to start at the top, competing with seasoned professionals. These people have been perfecting their writing talents for decades. Take your time, develop your writing skills, and earn writing credits from the small presses first. It's better to sell an article to a small magazine and receive only $50 than it is to not make a sale to a large magazine and receive nothing.

SELLING TO MAGAZINES

Most beginning writers approach the magazine market by writing an article on a subject which is of interest to them, and then go around searching for a publisher, much like you would do for a book. Unfortunately, this is the worst way to get an article published. Although many small publications will readily accept and publish unsolicited manuscripts, most consumer and trade publications will not.

Like book publishers, magazine publishers are besieged with submissions. Because they have so much material available to them, they are highly selective. For this reason your chances of getting an unsolicited manuscript published are remote. Whether you contact a small or large publication, always send publishers a query letter first, even *before* you write the article.

The following five steps are those which professional writers use to get their articles published. Preparing your material like a professional will give you the best opportunity for publication.

Step One

Choose a general subject which is of interest to you. This should be a subject you would enjoy studying and writing about. A saying commonly repeated by editors is "write what you know." This is good advice you should follow. Pick a subject you know about or would like to learn about. The more you know about a particular subject and the more you are interested in the subject, the better job you will do writing about it. Many first time authors write on a subject they are very familiar with and are successfully published. With encouragement from their first successful publication, they attempt to write on other topics which they are less experienced with, but fail to interest editors and wonder why. You might, for example, consider writing a piece on "Real Estate Investment in Rural Areas," but if you don't know anything about real estate and don't care much about it, you probably shouldn't even try to write such an article. The best writing is produced from enthusiastic writers. If you can't get enthused about a topic, it will show in your writing and will probably be unsalable.

Step Two

Read and study your chosen topic. If you have an interest in a particular area, you probably already have subscriptions to magazines on the topic. If not, subscribe to them or go to the library and read them. Use *Writer's Market* and other reference sources and make a list of all publications within your particular subject area and keep it for future reference. Study these magazines to get an idea of what types of articles are published and what publishers are looking for. Look for popular trends, controversies, and subjects of most interest.

Step Three

Choose a specific topic to write about. Ideas will come to you as you read about your chosen subject. Do some preliminary research on your chosen topic to determine if you can find enough material to write a salable article. Make an outline of your proposed article to see if you can adequately develop and write it. Do not write the article yet.

Step Four

Write a query letter describing your article idea and state your qualifications (writing credits, experience, training, etc.). Keep the letter to no more than one page if possible. Address your letter to the proper editor by name. Names can be found in *Writer's Market* or in the masthead of the magazine. A letter addressed to simply "Editor" is a sure sign of an amateur. You may give an estimated time when you feel you could have the article completed. Spend some time composing your letter and reread it to eliminate any spelling or grammatical errors. Submit your query to every publication on the list you previously made. Wait for a response. If you send the queries out together, let the editor know that it is a simultaneous submission. Check with *Writer's Market* as some publications dislike multiple submissions.

Step Five

If one of the publications accepts your idea and assigns you to write the article, you've been successful. You then write the article and submit it. If you sent out simultaneous submissions and more than one is interested in your article, choose one and aim your article that publication's readers.

Allow about six weeks for all publications to respond. If some of the publications do not respond to your initial mailing, resubmit your query and mention that this is a follow-up letter. Always include a stamped self-addressed envelope for a response.

What happens if none of the publications initally accept your article idea? You don't have to throw away your idea and start all over again at step one. Keep your idea and take the next step toward your goal of publication. Don't take rejections personally. Your writing is a product you are selling. The editor simply has chosen not to purchase your product. Change your product and try again.

You don't need to choose an entirely different topic. Keep your original topic but change it slightly by giving it a new focus, or new slant, and resubmit it to all of the publications on your list. Keep revising and resubmitting until you make a sale.

Let me give you an example. Let's say you chose hunting and fishing as your general topic of interest. You've made a list of all publications that print articles related to hunting and fishing and studied the articles in them. You chose a specific topic such as "Bass Fishing on the Yellowstone River." Submit query letters to the publications on your list. If all of them reject your initial proposal, revise your topic slightly to something such as "Trout Fishing on the Yellowstone River" and try again, and keep trying until you sell the article. You may eventually end up writing an article titled "Dry Fly Fishing on the Snake River," but you will make the sale. This is the process you should use. It will save you time and get you the best results.

Study the Markets

As I have mentioned, the worst thing you can do is write an article and then go looking for a publication willing to buy it. Likewise, you wouldn't necessarily send the same query letter to every editor either. Slant the letter to interest each editor.

The primary reason most article ideas are rejected by editors is because the writer did not take the time to study the magazine's needs. The articles are not in harmony with the magazine's focus and readership.

Every publication is different. Each looks for a particular voice, style, and viewpoint. Even two similar magazines could have very different readerships. For example, two magazines on health and fitness could cater to different age groups, one for young audiences and the other for more mature readers, or they could cater to different income levels or attitudes. Although articles in the two publications may be similar in concept, they would have a distinct focus. You need to become familiar enough with the publications you submit material to so you can slant your articles to the readers' interests. In order to do this, you will need to study the publications before submitting anything to them. By studying them I don't just mean reading the articles. You need to carefully examine the entire publication so you can get a clear idea of the type of people who read it.

Start by looking at the cover. The most obvious way of determining the focus of a magazine is by analyzing the cover. The cover design and featured articles advertise the magazine's image and will give you an idea of the type of people who read it. The next most important element you should look at are the featured articles. Try to determine the interests and personalities of the people they were written for.

Don't restrict your reading to just the articles; read the editorials and other material. Make a point of reading the editor's column, letters to the editor, and any special short features. These will contain valuable insights into the character of the readership. Also, you should study the ads. Since advertisers pay a pretty penny to advertise, they carefully choose the publications they advertise in. What type of products or services are advertised? What can you say about the type of people who would buy these products and services? A magazine that carries ads depicting families and children would suggest a readership interested in family unity and concerned about the issues and threats to a stable family life. These are the type of people you would be writing your article for.

As you study the publications, you should also analyze what specific topics the magazines are most interested in. What topics seem to get the most coverage? What trends are currently hot? What controversies, problems, and viewpoints stir up the most interest? The letters to the editor section is a gold mine of this type of information. As you study, use your imagination and seek intriguing topics which would be of interest to the magazine's readers.

Slant your query letter to each magazine rather than sending the same letter to all. Emphasize points you believe coincide with the focus of the publication. When you write the article, slant your material to that viewpoint. If the editors believe your article is not written with the right viewpoint it could still be rejected.

Don't send a 10,000 word article to a magazine that never publishes anything larger than 2,000 words. Learn what size articles are appropriate for the magazine you are interested in and write your articles within those limits. Most magazine editors will give you a word limit. This isn't just a recommendation, it is a requirement you must closely follow. If you add more, they will cut something out. If your article falls short, they may come back and ask you to write more. Stay as close to the requested length as possible. Magazines have a precise amount of space to fill and all articles must fit the available space.

WORKING WITH MAGAZINE EDITORS

If the editor thinks your idea has some promise, but you are an inexperienced writer, he may ask you to write the article or a portion of it on speculation, that is, without a promise to buy the finished article. That way he can see how well you do. He may also ask you for an outline of the proposed article before he'll actually give you the go-ahead to write it.

You should have made a basic outline of your proposed article before you wrote the query letter. Your initial research laid the foundation of the information you would include and how you would structure the article. Using your original outline as a guide, you could write a new outline geared specifically to any publication which shows interest in your article idea.

The outline should be double-spaced and limited to about two or three pages. In the outline tell precisely how the article will be structured, how you will approach the subject, what people you plan to interview, and what research or studies you will make, etc.

Editors want to know how much thought you have put into your article idea. Having a detailed outline shows them you have done some initial research and can complete the article. This is what editors want to see. If you are new to the editor, whether you've been published or not, the editor will want to know if you are capable of writing an acceptable article. If he doesn't request an outline from an unknown writer, how is he to know if the author is capable of writing a satisfactory story? Many aspiring magazine writers have come to editors with great story ideas and gotten the assignment to write the article only to find that writing it was not as easy as expected, and consequently the article died. This is a waste of time for an already busy editor and creates problems in scheduling articles for the publication. Your outline shows the editor you know what you're doing and can do the job. If you get an assignment to write your proposed article, you should work within the limits the editor gives. These may include article length, submission deadline, and suggestions on how to present the information. When you send in your article, include a cover letter briefly explaining the article and reminding him of previous correspondence. In the time you spent writing the article, the editor could have talked to literally hundreds of other writers about their material, and you or your assignment may not be immediately remembered.

After your manuscript has been submitted to the editor, it will go through an editing process. The editor will make corrections, additions, deletions, and changes as he sees fit. He may do some extensive rewriting if he feels it necessary, or he may return it to you to rewrite. If serious changes are considered necessary, the editor will usually consult with you about a revision. A good editor will only make changes when absolutely necessary. You've got to trust the editor. The changes he suggests or makes are based on his experience and knowledge of the magazine and its readers.

Some of the larger publications will send you a galley proof of your article to check before publication. Most, however, will not. The galley is beneficial, as it will show you what editing changes were made to your article before publication. If you have concerns, spot errors, or have a problem with how your article was edited, you can talk to the editor about it. Although the editor has the right to make the final decision as to what gets published, if you have serious concerns, something can generally be worked out between you. At least you will understand the reasons for the editor's changes.

After sending the editor your manuscript, you may not hear back from him until after the article has been published. By then it is obviously too late to make changes and you will have to live with the editor's decisions. Usually this does not cause a problem, however, sometimes you may be annoyed at having something changed. There's not much you can do about it. At any rate, unless the editor made some serious errors in the editing process, it is best not to complain. After all, his job is to edit the material he buys and he has that right.

Sometimes after you have written the article and submitted it, the editor will reject it. Just because the publication gave you the go-ahead to write the article does not necessarily mean they will publish it, or that you will get paid the stated fee. The completed article will still have to be reviewed and accepted. If the article is well written and fits their needs, chances are it will be published. However, any number of things can occur that will prevent the article from being published. The primary reason is that the author simply could not present the material in a way satisfactory to the editor. If the editor is still interested in using the article he will have the author make revisions. Sometimes he will cancel the assignment. Another reason for not publishing the article is that the editor decides the subject is not currently of great enough interest. Some topics may be of interest one day, but not a few months later. Even in the short time it takes to write the article, the readers' interest may have changed. Current events and trends change at an unpredictable pace. Another reason is that a competitor may have recently printed a very similar article.

If your article is canceled, you will normally receive a kill fee, which is only a percentage of the original amount promised (typically about 20 percent). This is a sum paid by the publication to compensate you for your time in writing the article.

Even if your article is accepted and paid for, it still may not be printed. Oh sure, you've got the money, but you miss out on seeing your work in print and being able to use it as a writing credit because it wasn't actually used. This happens to maybe as much as 10 percent of the articles accepted. Most magazines have a set limit in pages, and the amount of article space is determined by the amount of advertising space sold. Since magazines make the majority of their profit from advertising, ad copy gets priority over articles. But the magazine must be prepared with enough articles if advertising allows. For this reason some articles will inevitably be delayed or even cut entirely. Some articles, which are not particularly timely, can be held for years before they are published. I've heard of writers who have had articles appear in print as much as four years after submission.

A more agonizing experience is to have the article accepted, but with terms of pay-on-publication. This means the author will be paid the amount offered when the article is actually published. Many articles accepted under this term of payment are delayed or never printed for one reason or another. In the latter case, not only do you not get into print but you don't get paid either. Often, the article ages (becomes outdated) so it is unsalable to other publications. Many publications pay only on publication. You might be able to negotiate for payment on acceptance. If you are a relatively inexperienced writer, the publisher may not be easily persuaded to modify his offer. If you are a published author and have proven your ability to get published, you have more leverage to work with when negotiating with a publisher and can more readily find another publisher if necessary.

TIPS ON ARTICLE WRITING

Choose a specific topic. "The Grand Canyon," for example, is such a broad topic that entire books can be written on it. Hundreds of articles can be written about various aspects of the Grand Canyon, all of which could have distinctly different markets. An article titled "Rock Climbing in the Grand Canyon" would appeal to people who subscribe to a rock climbing magazine, but would hardly be appropriate for a family oriented magazine. On the other hand, "Family Recreational Activities in the Grand Canyon" would be suitable. Other article topics such as "How to Get a Summer Job at the Grand Canyon" and "The Best Hiking Trails in the Grand Canyon" are a couple examples of specific subjects that would appeal to different magazines.

For your article to be meaningful and salable, you need to give it a direction or focus by adding a viewpoint or theme. What is the purpose of the article? What does the article accomplish? Make your overall message clear. If your article is titled "The Best Non-Alcoholic Party Drinks," your aim could be to provide exciting alternatives to alcohol and consequently avoid all the adverse side effects alcohol consumption causes. Your article should make readers think and motivate them into action. After reading about nonalcoholic drinks, readers should be excited about trying them at their next party or group gathering or even just for fun with the family.

Viewpoint puts life into an article and makes it exciting and interesting. Without it the article is nothing more than a report. This may be all right for a technical journal, but not for most consumer magazines or even trade publications. Express your opinion and back it up with facts, personal experiences, and anecdotes which illustrate the points you make.

Include specific details and descriptions to illustrate and verify what you say. Don't just say the Grand Canyon is very deep. Tell exactly how deep it is, and add colorful, personal descriptions. Don't just say, "Many people are killed by drunk drivers." Give facts and figures.

Organize your article. Make it follow a logical path from one point to the next. Connect different thoughts by smooth transitions, and remain on a single theme. Begin with a lead paragraph that will grab the reader's interest. If the story starts out slowly, few people will read it. Use a lead that will spark readers' interest and curiosity and involve them in reading your story. When writing your lead paragraph, however, don't use misleading statements or something irrelevant to the rest of your story.

Keep the story exciting, eliminate cliches, repetitive phrases, and words. Proofread it several times to catch spelling, grammar, and other errors. Make sure your facts are correct. If you follow all of these guidelines, you will be on the right path to publication.

Let others read your articles and get feedback from them. If there is a writers' group in your area, it could be helpful to join them so you can evaluate each other's work. Also, continue to improve your writing skills by taking creative writing and journalism classes at local schools and colleges. Practice and feed-back from others will help you improve your skills. Take the opportunity.

HOW TO WRITE QUERY LETTERS

Simply stated, a query letter is a brief but detailed letter written to interest an editor in your article. Sending a query letter first is better for both you and the publisher. The publisher isn't bur-dened with a multitude of manuscripts he doesn't want, and for you, it takes less postage, money, and time to send out query letters than complete manuscripts.

The query is a single-spaced business letter usually limited to one page. It should be clean and neat. Typed, not hand written. What you write must be accurate, free of spelling and grammati-cal errors, and written in an interesting and compelling style. If you can't convince the editor to read your material, it does not matter how good your manuscript is—it won't be read. The query is a sample of your writing ability and style. A well written query suggests you can produce a quality manuscript. Writing a good query letter is a vital step to getting published.

Don't try to be cute or funny. Just give the facts. Publishing and writing is a business. Editors are professionals and expect those they work with to be the same.

Format

When you send a query letter, you are in a sense sending a sales letter to a business in an attempt to sell a product—your writing. The query should be set up in a businesslike format. On the letter you should have your full name, address, phone number, and date. You should also include the name of the editor you are submitting it to, the company name, and address.

Most business letters use a block style format as show on the next page. If you have a business name and printed statio-nery, the name and address are usually positioned somewhere at the top of the sheet. If you don't have printed stationery, you

Janice Williams
Freelance Writer
132 Main Street
Alief, Texas, 77902
(713) 546-7483

July 22, 19—

Linda Roe
Healthy Living Magazine
101 Broadway
New York, NY 10011

Dear Ms. Roe:

Each year one million Americans are diagnosed as having cancer. As yet, there is no sure cure for this disease. Recent studies, however, by Prescott University and the American Cancer Foundation have demonstrated that certain nutrients in our foods play a significant roll in cancer prevention.

I would like to propose an article for you which explains the new breakthroughs that researchers have discovered in cancer prevention and how to benefit from them. The article would describe the types of foods which are high in cancer-fighting nutrients and how to prepare this food to obtain the greatest nutritional value. Readers will also learn how to counter cancer-causing food additives, how to boost the body's immunity against cancer, and how hereditary factors leading to cancer often can be overcome.

I am very familiar with the research being done in cancer prevention. I have a Master of Science degree in biomedical technology and have assisted in cancer research at Alief Medical Hospital where I am employed. I have had articles published in <u>Prevention Magazine</u> and <u>Health and Fitness</u>.

I can have a 2,000 word article finished by August 30. If you would be interested in this article, please let me know. A self-addressed stamped envelope is enclosed for your convenience. This is a simultaneous query.

Yours truly,

Janice Williams

Example of a query letter.

may type your name and address centered at the top of the sheet. When typing your query or any correspondence, use this format or that shown on pages 41-43.

Address

You should address the letter to a specific editor. You can find these names in directories such as *Writer's Market* or *Literary Market Place*. If you don't know the submissions editor's name, call the company and ask for it. Be sure to get the spelling correct. Editors in the publishing industry move frequently, either by changing positions within a company or by switching firms. For this reason, you may want to verify the name of the editor before sending your material. Many publishers, particularly the larger companies, will return your material without even looking at it if the person you addressed it to is no longer with the company. A call will eliminate this problem.

You may also simply address the letter to the "submissions editor." If the company publishes different types of material, you may want to be more specific by writing "fiction submissions editor," "humor submissions editor," etc. A letter addressed to a specific person will undoubtedly receive more attention than one that is not. After all, if the sender knows the editor by name, he may have had previous dealings with him so his package will receive more attention. Also, mail rooms of the larger publishing houses sort mail and deliver the packages to the editors; sometimes they open the packages first. A name and address on the cover letter will ensure that it reaches the right person.

In the salutation of the letter, use Mr. or Ms., not the editor's first name. If gender cannot be determined use the full name (i.e., Dear Leslie Smith). Once you have corresponded for a while you may begin your salutation with the editor's first name, but usually only after he begins calling you by your first name.

Opening

The opening is probably the most important part of your letter. You make your first impression by how you present yourself and describe your article idea. As the editor reads your letter, he will be making judgements about you and your work. You need to convey a positive and professional tone.

A key to making a good impression with the editor is to present yourself in a professional manner. Like an intriguing novel with an enticing beginning, you need to start your letter with a strong opening. You need to spark the editor's interest and make him want to learn more. You might consider an opening similar to the one you use in your manuscript since it should have been written to interest and entice readers to read the rest of the article. Your opening paragraph should briefly describe the subject of the article so the editor knows what category it belongs to and what the article is about.

Description of the Subject
The next paragraph briefly outlines the structure and content of the article. State some facts and mention people you intend to interview, if it is relevant to your article. Give the editor enough information to make him want to know more.

Qualifications
Mention any special training or experience that qualifies you to write the article. If the article is on health and fitness, let him know you have a college degree in health, physical therapy, or whatever, and describe the experience you have had in the field. If your article is on prospecting for gold, your qualifications might be the number of years of experience you've had, important discoveries you've made, or new techniques you invented that have proved successful or that have brought you recognition from colleagues. You may also mention special awards that indicate your achievements.

Writing Experience
If you have had any of your writing published, mention that fact and tell who published it. It doesn't have to be a best selling book or even be published by a large company. It could be a nonpaying publication; it doesn't matter how much you were paid, or if you were even paid at all.

If you are or have been a staff writer for a publication, you should mention this fact. It may also be included as part of your qualifications if it relates to the subject you are writing about. You may mention that you were a winner or finalist to a noted literary contest. But don't bother to tell the editor you won a writing contest in high school or successfully completed a writer's workshop or conference; this type of information means very little to the editor.

If you do not have any writing experience, don't call attention to the fact. Let the editor assume, based on your professional presentation, that you are an experienced writer. Don't mention projects you are or have been working on if they have not been published. Saying you have written five novels which are currently unpublished says that you like to write but don't have the skill to get published.

You will want to keep your list of qualifications and writing credits to one or two paragraphs. If you have more to tell than can be stated in this amount of space, put it on a separate sheet of paper. This is usually called an author bio—short for biography. Here is where you can explain in detail your work and professional experience which qualify you to write the article. List writing you have had published, who published it, and when. The bio should be written in third person as if someone else was talking about you. This is not a resume. Include only relevant accomplishments. Do not mention personal data which has no direct connection to the material you are submitting.

Closing

In your closing paragraph you may include an offer to send the manuscript. You may specify the date the manuscript can be completed. Also, as a courtesy, indicate if you are sending query letters to other publishers.

MANUSCRIPT PREPARATION

As a publisher, I receive hundreds of manuscripts. They come to me in an assortment of styles and formats. Some follow the guidelines for proper manuscript preparation, many do not. The appearance of the manuscript, either consciously or subconsciously, affects my attitude toward it. Editors will judge a work by its looks before they even read it. Some editors will reject a manuscript without reading it simply because it is messy or was not typed in the proper format. A manuscript should never be rejected for this reason—it is a very simple matter to type and present the manuscript properly.

Although the appearance and structure of a manuscript says a lot about the author, *slight* variations in the format are perfectly acceptable. There is no *one* correct way to prepare a manuscript. A publisher will not reject a manuscript simply because you inserted an extra space below the title. Publishers are not that picky. Professional writers use somewhat different formats, but their manuscripts all contain the needed information and are easy to read. I will describe to you how to properly prepare your manuscript in a neat and professional-looking format. I recommend that you follow the standardized format I present as closely as possible. Too much deviation will only advertise yourself as an amateur and reduce your chances of getting published.

A manuscript which doesn't follow proper format signals to the editor that the writer is an amateur, has no publishing credits, lacks knowledge of the publishing and writing profession, and is too lazy to learn the proper submission procedures. This suggests the writing in the manuscript will be second-rate.

It really puzzles me why someone will spend months and even years of hard work researching and writing a book or a article, and spend no time in finding out how to prepare and submit it to a publisher.

If you can present your work in a professional manner, I guarantee your manuscript will pass the first round of rejections and be given more careful consideration from an editor.

Professional Appearance
The appearance of your manuscript and accompanying materials is one factor which you can easily handle professionally. You are competing with professional writers so you should make

your material appear as attractive as possible. When you write a manuscript, you are actually producing a product that you will eventually try to sell. If you were a buyer, would you want to buy a product that is obviously inferior or of poor workmanship? No, of course not. Editors don't either. If your submission looks amateurish, the editor will not take you seriously. If, on the other hand, you present your material in a professional manner, even though you are yet unpublished, the editor will treat your material with the respect due to a professional.

Because of the multitude of material they receive, editors' time is precious and they like material that is easy to read. For this reason, handwritten manuscripts are totally unacceptable. Dot-matrix computer printouts are usually undesirable and many editors won't accept them unless they are of letter-quality. Use a good typewriter, word processor, or computer that can produce letter-quality characters. Laser printers do an excellent job, and although not necessary, they do give a good impression.

Avoid using old, worn-out typewriters that blur the letters, fill ink in the loops (i.e., d, e, o), or can't type in a consistently straight line. Get the typewriter fixed, buy a new one, or have someone type it for you—but make it neat. Do not cross out or put XXs through typographical errors and avoid too many corrections made by hand with a pen. A few errors can be corrected with correction tape or fluids. If there are too many errors, retype the page! Careless writing is produced by careless authors.

A great manuscript will go unread if the type style is not easy to read. Don't use all capital letters, cursive, or any other fancy type style. With computers and laser printers, it is easy to use fancy fonts, but don't. The easier the manuscript is to read, the better chance you have of getting it read. Use a standard type style for all of your submission materials.

If you print from a computer onto fanfold paper with tractor edges, strip off the feeder strips and separate the pages before you send them. Make sure the characters are clear and dark enough to be easily read.

Some publishers will accept electronic submissions (over a modem or on diskettes). However, do not send a submission over a modem or fax unless you are specifically invited to do so by the editor.

Manuscript Format

Use 8½ x 11-inch white paper for your manuscript. Type on only one side of the sheet. Do not staple the sheets together. You may use a paper clip to hold them together if you desire. If you are submitting an article or short story, a cover sheet or title page is not necessary. You may use a title page for book-length manuscripts.

All the margins on the page should be 1 to 1¼ inches. At the top of the first page of the manuscript you will put important information on yourself and the work. This information should be single-spaced. In the upper left hand corner type your name (use your real name and not a pseudonym), mailing address, phone number where you can be reached during the day, and your social security number. The social security number is included for tax purposes. The publisher is required to report all payments to the IRS. The number is provided as a convenience to him. Although many publishers may reject the manuscript, the one who accepts it needs the information.

In the upper right corner of the first page, indicate the approximate number of words in the manuscript. This is important because publishers have a strict range they must work within. Count the number of words in 10 full lines of the manuscript. Divide this number by 10 to find the average words per line. Multiple this number by the number of lines on a page to find the words per page. Multiply the number of words per page by the total number of pages to get your word count.

Indicate what rights you are offering for sale below the word count. Normally you would offer first serial rights, which means the publication has the right to publish the article for the first time in any periodical. You may also put a copyright notice under the rights statement if you want. This is done by typing the word "copyright" or the symbol "©" followed by the year and your name. A hand written copyright symbol is acceptable. If you are using a title page, do not number it or include it in the total page count. Do not number the first page but include it in the page count.

Come down the page one-third of the way and type the title. The title should be centered and in all capital letters. Double space after the title and type "by," double space again and type your name or pseudonym. The line with your name is referred to as your byline. If you are going to make this a title page, then it is complete. If you are not using a separate title page, drop down two double spaces below your byline and indent five spaces from the left margin. Now, begin the body of your manuscript. The body of the manuscript should be double-spaced. For each paragraph indent five spaces.

Type your name and page number on every page after the first. This is called the slug line. The slug line will keep pages in order and keep them from being mixed with someone else's material. In the upper left corner type your last name, a dash, and the page number. The title of your manuscript could be typed on this line or beneath this if you desire. If you are using a pseudonym, type your real name, followed by your pen name in parentheses and the page number—for example, Clemens (Twain) - 2. Drop down two double spaces and resume typing.

After the last sentence at the end of the manuscript, if it is a work of fiction, drop down three double spaces and center the words "The End" to indicate the end of the manuscript. If it is nonfiction, use ### or the symbol - 30 - which signifies the same thing. On the following two pages are examples of the first and last pages of an sample manuscript set up in proper format.

MAILING SUBMISSIONS

When sending an editor your manuscript, use an envelope that is large and strong enough to hold it. If your manuscript is only five pages or less, you may fold it in thirds and send it in a #10 (business-size) envelope. For manuscripts over five pages, use 9 x 12-inch envelopes.

Susan Bly
443 Park Avenue
New York, NY 10011
(212) 543-4433
SS# 535-89-9847

3,000 words
First Serial Rights
© 1993 by Susan Bly

THE FRONTIERSMAN WHO BECAME PRESIDENT

by

Susan Bly

When Andrew Jackson came upon the stage of American political affairs as the seventh President of the United States, a new era began in the history of the country. The control of the government by the "Virginia dynasty" and the Adams family was at an end, and the rule of the frontier had begun.

As a specimen of the new type of American manhood which was now to dominate the country, no better person could be found than Andrew Jackson. The son of Scotch-Irish parents who had settled in the frontier wilderness of the Carolinas shortly before his birth, he displayed the characteristics of the Waxhaw region in which he was born and

Example of the first page of a manuscript.

Bly — 11

During the eight years which followed Jackson's retirement, the hard times which came upon the country in 1837 hurt him financially and also disturbed his peace of mind. But they did not destroy his popularity. Admirers named their children for him and asked for his autograph; and so many wrote to request a lock of his hair that he kept the clippings whenever he had it cut. Neither Washington nor Jefferson enjoyed the popularity that "Old Hickory" did, nor have many presidents since his day possessed to such a degree the love and confidence of the majority of the people. He died at his estate, The Hermitage, near Nashville, Tennessee, on June 8, 1845, and was buried in the garden.

-30-

Example of the last page of a manuscript.

When sending a manuscript, make sure it has the correct postage. I get envelopes all the time stamped "Postage Due" because the sender did not take the time to properly weigh and stamp it. They are sent back to the senders unopened. If you want a response from the publisher, you must include a self-addressed stamped envelope (SASE). Whether you are sending a one page query letter or a full manuscript, you need to include a return envelope and postage.

Send an envelope large enough to accommodate the material you want returned, preaddressed with stamps in place. If you are sending your material in a #10 envelope, send a business-size return envelope. A #10 return envelope should be folded in thirds. You could also use a slightly smaller #9 envelope which will fit into the #10 envelope without folding. If you are submitting material requiring a larger envelope, include an envelope large and sturdy enough to hold it. A 9 x 12-inch envelope or mailer can be folded in half.

You may decide you don't need to have your manuscript returned. However, you still want to receive a response from the editor. If all you want is a response, all you need to send is a business-size SASE. The manuscript, if not accepted, is then discarded. In your cover letter you may indicate that the manuscript need not be returned.

If you inquire with any publisher outside the country, you cannot use postage stamps on your return envelopes. Stamps on the return envelope must be from the country in which it is mailed. A Canadian publisher, for example, must have Canadian stamps and these are only sold in Canada. What you can do is include an International Reply Coupon (IRC) with your envelope. You can purchase IRCs at any post office. The publisher exchanges them for postage at his post office. Postage rates are different in foreign countries, so make sure you buy enough IRCs for the return.

Since postage out of the country can be very expensive, especially for heavy manuscripts, it is best to send only a return envelope and postage and let the publisher keep the manuscript.

You may want to include photos with your manuscript.

Don't send your only copies. To prevent undue damage, reinforce your mailing envelope with cardboard inserts. Write on the outside of the envelope "PHOTOS—DO NOT BEND." You may also use a heavy cardboard envelope, available at packaging or photography supply stores.

Always make a copy of your manuscript, illustrations, and any documents that may accompany them. Once this material leaves your possession, you have no control over what happens to it. It may be lost or destroyed in the mail, misplaced by an editor, or accidently thrown out by a member of the office staff.

CHAPTER 7

LITERARY SERVICES

With the rising popularity of the small press industry over the past few years, opportunities for copy editors and proofreaders, as well as other readers, have greatly increased. If you have the qualifications to provide literary services, you could have a very successful and enjoyable career. In this chapter I will focus my attention specifically on editors, proofreaders, technical readers, and literary critics.

As a publisher, I receive many manuscripts from authors, most all of which are rejected. One of the primary reasons I reject manuscripts is because the authors do not bother to have their material proofread, edited, or critiqued by a competent reader. Editorial problems and errors are rampant in most of the manuscripts I receive. Other publishers complain of the same problem. Consequently, these writers' chances of getting published are slim. Many professional writers have learned to use the services of editors and proofreaders, and they have succeded in getting their work published.

I know of one best selling author who has as many as five independent readers go over his manuscripts before he sends them to his publisher. If a person successful enough to have had several best selling novels to his credit feels the need to have his writing proofread this many times, then novice writers should seriously consider it. Without a doubt the writer who has all of the problems ironed out of his manuscript before sending it to the publisher will greatly increase his chances for publication.

PROOFREADING

When you read for pleasure do you frequently run across typographical errors and misspelled words? Are these errors so obvious they appear to jump up out of the page at you? If you can easily spot errors in grammar, punctuation, and misused or misspelled words, you may have a natural talent for proofreading.

All businesses compose and disseminate various types of literature. These include in-house publications, newsletters, annual reports, advertising copy, sales literature, catalogs, business letters, and the like. One of the major avenues in which customers, clients, and business associates form opinions about a company is through the literature it produces. For this reason the company's written materials must be as error free and professional-looking as possible. To do this, businesses use proofreaders and copy editors. Many businesses hire full-time editors and proofreaders; others routinely hire freelancers.

Most businesses don't use qualified readers because they depend on secretaries and other office staff. These people, however, are often not sufficiently qualified to do this type of work. They may catch obvious errors, but there is much more to proofreading and editing than spotting simple typographical errors.

Some people depend on computer software programs, designed to check for spelling and grammatical errors, for their editing needs. But such programs should not be a substitute for having material proofread. The computer programs will catch simple errors, but pass over words spelled correctly but misplaced or incorrectly used in the text. It takes a human to catch these types of errors.

Even writers should never depend on their own proofreading. They become so familiar with their own material that they tend to see only what they want or expect to see. I know this through experience. I have read my own short copy over and over looking for errors and then hand it to someone else who readily points out typos I missed which should have been obvious. This sort of thing happens to all writers.

Many businesses don't realize they need qualified readers and rely on the methods mentioned above. They can, however, be persuaded to use proofreading services if shown the importance of it.

How to Proofread

Proofreading involves more than simply reading and noting typographical errors. The type of problems proofreaders need to catch and correct include typographical, grammar, spelling, and other mechanical errors, as well as factual errors and inconsistency in style.

A proofreader's job is to correct all of the writer's errors without creating any additional ones. The proofreader is usually the last person to check a text before it is published or delivered to its intended reader. The proofreader must catch as many remaining errors as possible. No matter whose error it might be initially, the proofreader is eventually responsible. If too many errors remain after you have proofread the material, you will have dissatisfied clients and lose business. Although it may be nearly impossible to catch every single error in lengthy projects (i.e., book-length manuscripts), you need to do as good a job as you possible can.

Proofreaders employed within companies frequently make their initial reading by comparing the original edited text with the typeset proof copy. This method is used to catch errors the typesetter may have made, as well as errors the editor may have missed. The proofreader compares the original text (referred to as the dead copy) to the proof (called the live copy, since it is the one being corrected). Each word is compared throughout the entire text. This is a slow and tedious process for one proofreader to perform. At times two proofreaders are used—one reading the dead copy and the other following along and correcting the live copy. Full-time proofreaders who work as company employees sometimes work this way. Although a freelance proofreader might be asked to do some comparison proofreading, most of the time the work will involve reading only the proof copy (also known as dry reading). Since the primary concern in this book is freelance proofreading, I will focus on dry reading.

To do a good job proofreading you will need to devote your full attention and concentration to the material you are reading. Work in a quiet room without distractions or interruptions. Do not listen to the radio or TV. A quiet atmosphere will set up a good environment in which to concentrate and work effectively.

Do not try to finish jobs too quickly by reading faster than you normally do. You should read at a slow, comfortable pace. You need to look at every word in an effort to correct mechanical errors. You must also make an effort to understand what the author is saying so you can identify errors which are not mechanical, such as using a correctly spelled word in the wrong place or identifying a misplaced decimal point.

While you are working, take breaks as often as necessary to keep your mind fresh and alert. Some material you read may be uninteresting to you and you may become bored and consequently less attentive and productive. Frequent breaks will help fight fatigue and keep you from becoming lazy. Another way to make your job more interesting is to look at it as a game or a challenge and try to find as many errors as possible.

You should read each project at least twice, and more times if necessary. On one reading through the text, you should concentrate on content. Focus on what the author is saying rather than simply correcting mechanical errors. Read for consistency, word usage, sentence structure, repetition of thought, and the like. Reading the text once will give you an understanding of the author's writing style and purpose, enabling you to spot errors you might otherwise overlook. On another pass through the text, concentrate on mechanical errors such as capitalizations, punctuation, spelling, grammar, hyphenations, and word breaks. Of course, if you spot any of these errors on either pass, mark them so that you don't miss them the next time through. Read the material a third time, if necessary, to catch all errors.

Do not neglect to carefully read headings and subheadings. Often, simply because they are in larger or boldface type, they are assumed to be correct. But this is not necessarily so—read them carefully. Pay close attention to the table of contents, footnotes, bibliographies, index, tables, and charts. Also observe spacings between words and lines, margin sizes, position and spacing of headings, and page sequence. These are all part of proofreading.

When checking the bibliography, make sure all entries are alphabetical. Make sure entries in the index and table of contents match those in the text. A title on the contents page could be unknowingly altered on the chapter page. So could the page number. If, in the text, a reference is made to something on another page, check to make sure the number is accurate. These are common mistakes that occur when the text is converted from manuscript to final format.

Most people make the same types of mistakes, and you can catch these by paying particular attention to these areas. The most common types of errors are:

Misspelled words and names
Reversed or incorrect numbers in addresses and dates
Incorrect capitalization
Incorrect or missing punctuation
Nonagreement of subject and verb
Misusing words
Repeating words frequently
Omitting words

Tools for the Job
Every proofreader should have the proper tools to do the job. The most obvious tool of the proofreader is a marking pen. Use

a colored pen or pencil so the client can easily spot the corrections. It is very difficult for the client to search for corrections marked in black pen or pencil. Small marks such as the addition of a period, comma, or hyphen can go unnoticed and eventually uncorrected. So, make your marks easy to spot. Other materials every proofreader should have access to include: dictionary, grammar/punctuation book, style book, atlas, and thesaurus or synonym finder. Special dictionaries for specific professions, such as a foreign language dictionary, geological dictionary, or dictionary of legal terms, are helpful if you work in a specific discipline.

Editorial Style
There are certain rules of spelling, grammar, punctuation, capitalization, and the like that must be followed in order to maintain consistency within the language. In many instances there is more than one acceptable way to format the language. This is referred to as editorial style. A percentage figure, for example, may be written as "50%," "50 percent," or "fifty percent." All are correct, but only one should be used consistently within a single text. Businesses and industries try to maintain consistency by adhering to one set of standards. Many people, however, unknowingly use a mixture of the various styles, which you will be required to correct.

There are many published stylebooks, each of which are designed for a specific industry or type of writer. For example, the U.S. government has its own set of style standards that writers of government publications must follow. The newspaper industry has its own style standards. The medical profession has its own style preferences.

The most popular stylebook is *The Chicago Manual of Style,* used by academic and literary writers. There are several other stylebooks. Many publishers and other businesses have house styles of their own. Copy editors and proofreaders should ask clients which stylebook to follow. If none is preferred or mentioned, it is usually safe to follow the guidelines in *The Chicago Manual of Style*, but check with your client first. Often clients will not have a style preference although they may have a few preferences of their own. In most cases you c in follow *The Chicago Manual of Style* or other appropriate stylebook and incorporate any of the client's alternate preferences. All copy editors and proofreaders should use a *style sheet*. A style sheet is an organized listing of points of style to be remembered while reading. It is used for convenience as it saves time from searching through a stylebook every time a question of style arises. The style sheet consists of several sheets of paper, listing in alphabetical order points of style used for each particular client. You can't possibly remember all the points of style each client requires. The style sheet is a convenient reminder. You can create your first style sheet using the guidelines in the stylebook you use as your basic guide. Use variations of that style sheet to meet each client's needs and preferences.

A style sheet will be divided into the following sections, each of which I will explain.

Format
This is the physical appearance or layout of the text. It includes size of margins, line and word spacing, size of type, tabs, position of headlines and subheadings, etc.

Spelling and Capitalization
Know the client's preference on spelling and capitalization of proper nouns (names, places, organizations). For example, is a name spelled Leslie or Lesley? Ringling Bros. and Barnum & Bailey Circus writes their name this way and does not spell out the "Brothers" or the second "and." There are often two or more ways to correctly spell some words. For example, "blonde" could also be spelled "blond." Which does the client prefer?

Hyphenation
Words are often hyphenated when used either as compound adjectives (i.e., short-term) or compound nouns (i.e., strongman). However, they are not hyphenated when used together as an adjective and noun (short term, strong man). Another problem may arise with headings and capitalizations. Is the word after the

hyphen capitalized ("Low-pressure" or "Low-Pressure")? Some clients prefer hyphens while others do not. The key is to be consistent. If the copy isn't, check with the client for verification or follow the stylebook format.

Numerals

Numbers can be expressed as numerical figures or written out. Most often the numbers one through nine are written out, while 10 and above are given as figures. However, some authors may prefer writing out all numbers below 100 and using figures for the rest. Symbols accompanying numbers, such as dollar, cent, and percent signs, can be either expressed as symbols or written out (25%, 25 percent, twenty-five percent).

Dates

There are a variety of acceptable forms for dates. Some of the variations are: December 15, 1993; Dec. 15, 1993; 15 December 1993; 15 Dec. 1993; and 12/15/93. Apostrophes are not used with a full date (December 15, '93). If a comma precedes the year, a comma must follow, if it is not the end of the sentence. ("He was married on Feb. 22, 1963, and is proud of it." or "He was married on Feb. 22 1963 and is proud of it.") Century can be expressed as 20th century, 20th-century, twentieth century, or twentieth-century.

Possessives and Plurals

There is sometimes a choice on the use of apostrophes in treating possessives and plurals. Here are some examples:

John Williams' or John Williams's
Bill and Ted's adventure or Bill's and Ted's adventure
M's or Ms (A's, I's, U's but not As, Is, Us or as, is, us)
1900's or 1900s

Abbreviations

Many people are inconsistent in their use of abbreviations. There are several ways to abbreviate some words. Here are some examples:

Ill or IL; Cal., Calif., or CA
SE or S.E.
A.M. or a.m.
USA or U.S.A.; NCAA or N.C.A.A.
MD or M.D.; PhD or Ph.D.

An apostrophe is used whenever letters are left out of a
word. For instance, "do not" is abbreviated as "don't." The word
"and" is often condensed to 'n, n', or 'n'. An exception is the
word "until" which is not abbreviated as "'til" as you might
expect, but the accepted abbreviation is "till." A dash (—) or
ellipsis (...) is often incorrectly used to replace commas, semicolons, or end marks.

Foreign Words
All foreign words, except those which are frequently used in
English, should be italicized or underscored. Some examples of
foreign words commonly used in English that would not be
italicized are "resume," "ad nauseam," and "deja vu." These
words are common enough that most English speaking people
know their meanings and they are even included in English
dictionaries. Accent marks are an important element of many
foreign words. However, English speaking writers and editors
not accustomed to accents may misplace them, put them at the
wrong angle, or leave them off entirely. If the word is not
commonly used in English, it should have the accent marks and
the marks should be properly placed. As a general rule, if the
word is in the English dictionary don't italicize it.

Facts
You should keep track of facts and make sure that they are used
in a consistent manner throughout the text. For example, a
statement indicating there are 12 countries in the Europen Common Market, and then listing only eleven, would be a contradic-
tion that should be corrected. Calculations should also be checked
for accuracy. Don't glance quickly over facts and figures, read
them and make sure they make sense.

Trademarks, Servicemarks, and Copyrights

Trademarks and servicemarks are used by companies to show claim to certain words, names, or symbols which identify their company. The words are identified by the marks TM, SM, or ®. Companies are very protective of these names and symbols. If the marks aren't used consistently or the names are improperly used by others, the company could lose its right to them and they could become generic terms, which can be used by anybody. Advertising copy should always use the marks TM, SM, or ®. A footnote is commonly used to identify the company. In literary works the marks are not used, but the first letter of the words are capitalized, which serves the same purpose. The copyright symbol is used to show claim to literary or artistic works. When using quotations or material from a copyrighted source, it is necessary to give credit to this source, usually in a footnote.

Footnotes, Bibliographies, Indexes, Tables, and Graphs

These can be presented in a myriad of ways. Follow the format given by the client.

Special Treatment

A writer may intentionally deviate from accepted rules of grammar and punctuation, use a word differently, misspell, or even make up his own words to suit his own purposes. This is most common in advertising copy where the author is trying to draw reader's attention to something. Often ad writers use a play on words or spelling to make a product more noticeable. Conscious changes are also found in literary works. William Shakespeare introduced many new words into the English vocabulary this way.

Miscellaneous

There may be other style considerations which do not fit under any of these headings, such as in writing addresses, phone numbers, and terms associated with a particular profession or activity.

There you have it, the major categories you need in order to create your style sheet. On a sheet of blank paper, write each category described as a main heading. List your entries under each category in alphabetical order. Use as many sheets of paper as necessary. You should first read and study the stylebook you believe you will use most often. Create your first style sheet using this stylebook. At this point, your style sheet will be for practice and study more than anything else. As you begin working with clients who desire specific styles or have certain preferences, you will create style sheets for each of them.

Many of your clients will not indicate a particular style preference, and some will not even be aware that different styles exist. In such cases you will create a style sheet for them using your own standard style sheet and their text, contacting them for clarification whenever necessary. When you read the client's material for the first time, write down in the appropriate place on their style sheet every variation as you come to it. Although a client may only use your services one time, the style sheet will help you check consistency throughout the text. For clients who will use your services again, you will want to file the style sheet and refer back to it on subsequent projects.

Don't expect to keep track of all the style variations by memory alone! Many points of style can be remembered, but not everything. This is particularly true for proofreaders who have many clients. Too many amateur proofreaders plunge through texts without taking the time to create style sheets, and consequently miss many points that need correction. Style sheets are important and should be used in order for you to do a professional job.

Spelling Test

In order to be a good proofreader, you should have a good aptitude for spelling. The following list contains some commonly misspelled words. They are not particularly difficult, but represent a sample of the types of words you could encounter every day. Some of the words in this list are purposely misspelled. Can you identify them? Without using a dictionary, find the misspelled words and correct the spelling. Also, mark the words you believe are misspelled, but are not sure of the correct spelling. After completing this test, turn to page 98 for the answers.

abbreviate	ingenious
abcess	elixar
kalidoscope	acclimate
achieve	trechery
wiseacre	laryngitus
archaeology	masseuse
arrogence	marionette
mausoleum	baffle
barometer	nuisance
bizarre	orchestra
plainteff	Cadillac
calculas	humerous
calligraphy	polergeist
camoflage	potpouri
rhapsody	regergitate
cemetary	ceiling
clemancy	rheumetism
deodorant	sarcasm
desperate	silhouette
devastate	smorgasboard
discintegrate	theraputic
eccleastical	lariat
insedious	usery
exhilarate	vigalante
flamboyant	weasel
frugel	greivance
wierd	warewolf
hybrid	apparatus
impass	indiscreet
zucchini	xerox

Did you identify all of the misspelled words? Did you correctly spell those you corrected? A good proofreader should have been able to catch every misspelled word in this list. That does not mean you need to be able to spell every word in the English language or even know how to spell every word on this list. But you should have been able to at least identify all the misspelled words. Then use a dictionary to correct those you did not know how to spell or those which you needed to check. It really doesn't matter how many words you think might be wrong so long as you check them in the dictionary. It is much better to check the spelling on a correctly spelled word than to pass over an incorrect one.

If you were able to identify all or almost all of the misspelled words, you may have the eye for detail that is essential in proofreading. If you had trouble with this test, you would have difficulty working as a proofreader. I would like to point out that most publishers and many other business, require new freelance proofreaders and copyeditors to take a test before they are hired. The test would involve reading and correcting a sample text.

Proofreader's Marks

Proofreader's marks are shorthand notations for specific corrections. If you had to write out every correction it would be very time consuming and messy. Copy editors and proofreaders use the same marks in their editing. Copy editors commonly make corrections *within* the text while proofreaders indicate where errors are in the text, but make the corrections in the *margin*. The primary reason for this is that editors work with copy that is double-spaced, so there is room between the lines to make corrections. Proofreaders work with typeset proofs that are usually single-spaced.

Most of the proofreader's marks are standard and easily recognized by those who work with editors and proofreaders. Do not make up your own marks! That will only confuse the person reading the corrections. Learn and use the recognized marks. Although these marks are universally accepted, slight variations are sometimes used. This is particularly true within businesses which may use slightly different notations among its staff.

ANSWERS TO SPELLING TEST

The correct spelling to the words listed on page 96 are given below. Those words which were misspelled are flagged with an asterisk (*).

abbreviate	ingenious
abscess*	elixir*
kaleidoscope*	acclimate
achieve	treachery*
wiseacre	laryngitis*
archaeology	masseuse
arrogance*	marionette
mausoleum	baffle
barometer	nuisance
bizarre	orchestra
plaintiff*	Cadillac
calculus*	humorous*
calligraphy	poltergeist*
camouflage*	potpourri*
rhapsody	regurgitate*
cemetery*	ceiling
clemency*	rheumatism*
deodorant	sarcasm
desperate	silhouette
devastate	smorgasbord*
disintegrate*	therapeutic*
ecclesiastical*	lariat
insidious*	usury*
exhilarate	vigilante*
flamboyant	weasel
frugal*	grievance*
weird*	werewolf*
hybrid	apparatus
impasse*	indiscreet
zuchini*	Xerox*

Publishers, writers, and others in the literary field know and understand proofreader's marks. Some individuals and business people may not be very familiar with them, so it is wise to make a list of these marks and their definitions and give it to the client with the return of the corrected text. This way clients will not have to contact you for an explanation.

Standard proofreading marks you will have the most use for are listed in Table 1.

After the proofreader makes all necessary corrections, the text is returned to the client, who in turn gives it to the typest or typesetter to make the changes.

Proofreader's corrections are made in the margins exactly parallel to the line being corrected. See the following example.

(cap)   She lives in canada.

If more than one correction is needed on a line, begin proof marks at the far left side of the margin and separate each mark with a slant, working toward the right.

(cap)(tr)   Is joe going to send his in report on time?

If a correction is repeated, the marginal mark is followed by a slant and the number of repetitions circled.

(cap)(3)   She was a member of the united service organization.

Circling is used in the margins with proofreader's marks for clarification. Some confusion might occur between words of instruction to the typesetter and words that are to be added to the text. To avoid ambiguity, instructions to the typesetter are always circled. Words or letters that are to be added to the text are not. An exception to this rule is with periods and colons. Periods and colons are circled because they are so small they might otherwise be overlooked.

Circles are also used inside the text around a word or letter to be corrected. Never circle words that are to be typed or typeset

TABLE 1

Mark in Margin	Mark in Text	Explanation	Corrected Text
ℰ	the freelance readery	remove letter	the freelance reader
◠	the fre elance reader	close up	the freelance reader
stet	the freelance reader	let it stay	the freelance reader
lc	The freelance reader	lowercase letter	the freelance reader
lc/3	The Freelance Reader	lowercase letter	the freelance reader
lc	THE freelance reader	lowercase word	the freelance reader
rule	the freelance reader	underline	the freelance reader
ital	the freelance reader	italicize	the *freelance* reader
bf	the freelance reader	boldface type	the **freelance** reader
cap	the freelance reader	capitalize letter	The freelance reader
tr	hte freelance reader	transpose	the freelance reader
¶	She is the freelance reader. [Careful reading is necessary.	new paragraph	She is the freelance reader. Careful reading is necessary.
No ¶	She is the freelance reader. Careful reading is necessary.	same paragraph	She is the freelance reader. Careful reading is necessary.
#	the freelancereader	insert space	the freelance reader
?	the freelance readers	query to author	the freelance reader

Mark in Margin	Mark in Text	Explanation	Corrected Text
?	the freelance reader‸	insert question mark	the freelance reader?
⊙	the freelance reader‸	insert period	the freelance reader.
⊙	the freelance reader‸	insert colon	the freelance reader:
‸	the younger freelance reader	insert comma	the younger, freelance reader
‸	the freelance reader‸ the younger reader	add semicolon	the freelance reader; the younger reader
˅	the readerˇs work	add apostrophe	the reader's work
˅/˅	ˇthe freelance readerˇ	insert quotation marks	"the freelance reader"
⊂/⊃	the‸freelance‸reader	add parentheses	the (freelance) reader
⊥ / m	proofreading⌐as noted above	long dash (not hyphen)	proofreading—as noted above
=	the free‸lance reader	add hyphen	the free-lance reader
‖	‖the freelance reader	even out lines	the freelance reader
⊏	⊏ the freelance reader	move left	the freelance reader
⊐	the freelance reader ⊐	move right	the freelance reader
(SP)	③freelance readers	spell out word	three freelance readers

in the final copy. See the example below.

(SP)   He put ②socks in the dresser drawer.

A caret (∧) in the text is used to flag an insertion of a word, letter, and most punctuation marks. Draw the caret at the bottom of the line where the insertion is to be made. An inverted caret (∨) is placed inside the text to indicate the insertion of an apostrophe, quotation mark, superscript, or asterisk.

∧
s   He was very embarrased.
                          ∧

∖   ∨
∨   Lets go to school.

Always write legibly. Since space on the page is limited, there is a tendency to write very small. It is aggravating to typesetters to get proofread material that is difficult to read. A misspelled word that is illegibly corrected may be misspelled by the typesetter.

COPYEDITING

Copyediting is very similar to proofreading and, in some cases, there is a fine line of distinction between the two. Some proof-readers are so thorough their work is closer to that of a copy editor. Likewise, some copy editors focus their efforts so much on mechanical errors that they are little more than proofreaders. But there is a difference between the two. A copy editor's job includes everything a proofreader does, but goes one step further. In addition to making mechanical, factual, and format corrections, the copy editor corrects literary errors. These include correcting awkward sentence structure and clarifying sentences, words, or ideas not clearly expressed by the writer. The copy editor works on sentence structure, phrases, and choice of words to make the words flow smoother. Editors must read the text at least two or three times, and more if necessary.

Usually proofreaders will read material which is nearly finished and laid out in its final format. Copy editors, on the other hand, are the ones who make the initial corrections and preparations on manuscripts. The biggest difference resulting from making corrections at different stages of development of the text is that initially, the material will have more errors and require more corrections by the copy editor than the proofreader. However, since the material may not be in final format, it will be left up primarily to the proofreader to check the physical appearance and accuracy (spacings, margins, headings, page numbers, index, etc.).

Format

When working with many different types of businesses, you will be required to work with material in various formats. Some materials will be in manuscript form, while others will be in finished form. Writers and publishers will usually give you manuscripts that are double-spaced with ample margin space, but others unaccustomed to working with editors will often single-space their material. Recommend that your clients double space all material they give you. Also, have them leave a 1 to 1¼-inch margin on each side and the top and bottom. The extra space is necessary for you to make corrections and write comments.

Even though a text has been edited, after it has been laid out in final format it should be proofread or edited again before it is published or sent to its intended destination. Typographical, format, and even editing errors can occur after the initial editing.

Commentary

If you are editing, one thing that can make your editing more valuable to your clients is your comments throughout the text. This is not always true with proofreading as proofreaders generally are concerned only with correcting mechanical errors. Rather than just correcting typographical errors and other mistakes, take the time to make comments in the text. Some of these may be your opinions or observations, but all recommendations can be valuable. If something is confusing, say so. If you believe

THE PARTS OF A SENTENCE

The part of the sentence that represents what is talked about is called the *subject*. All the rest of the sentence, which asserts or *predicates* some-

(ital) thing, is called the predicate.

The complete subject of the sentence always

(¶) contains a noun or a pronoun, or a group of words used like a noun, which stands for the thing talked about. This is called the *subject substantive*. It may or may not have adjuncts or modifiers. in the   *(cap)* sentence "People who live in glass houses should

(") not throw stones, the word *people* is the subject substantive. It has as a modifier the clause *who live in glass houses*, showing which people are

(⊙) meant

The predicate of a sentence must always

(b) contain a ver. Sometimes this verb by itself says all we want to say about the subject; as "The water *boils*." But often we want to add to the meaning of the verb, to make it clearer more and definite; as   *(tr)* "Water *boils more rapidly if you make the fire hotter*." And again, certain verbs require other words to complete there meaning. Linking verbs,

(⤶) are such as *be, become*, take a *predicate* noun,

(※) pronoun, oradjective to complete their meaning.

A portion of a corrected text with proofreader's marks.

something could be expressed better, say so or rewrite it. Or, if you believe a statement may not be accurate or might be misleading, say so. Providing comments such as these will make you more valuable to the client and demonstrate to him that he needs your services. Whether or not he accepts your advice and comments is beside the point; the fact that you give him the option is beneficial. He may not have even considered some of the points you bring up, and therefore you can make a worthwhile improvement.

Technical corrections are the most important part of your editing, but commentary is an added benefit that will enhance your work and make you more useful to your clients.

A good practice to follow when you are editing or proofreading is when you come to an error that is not obvious, and apparently the writer did not know better, cite an authoritative source for the change (i.e., *The Chicago Manual of Style*). This shows the author it was not just your personal opinion that the change was necessary. Some clients will challenge you or ignore the correction if you don't. Giving the reference helps the client understand the reason for the change, and if he still prefers the original he will break the rule on purpose and not by ignorance.

Test Your Editing Skill

Some types of reading jobs can be done by just about anyone who can read. Proofreading and copyediting, however, require a firm knowledge and understanding of grammar, punctuation, spelling, sentence structure, mechanics, and the like. Do you have the skill to be a good proofreader or editor? Can you recognize dangling participles, misuse of colons and semicolons, poor transitions, or ambiguous statements? I have included a short test for you to experiment with. On the following two pages is a portion of an unedited manuscript. Read it and make all the necessary changes using proper proofreading marks as described in this chapter. You are given permission to make a photocopy of this page for this purpose without violating the copyright on this book. Do this exercise now before reading any further.

ARCHIMEDES (287-212 B.C.)

"Give me a place to stand and to rest my lever on," said Archimedes the ancient Greek mathematician and inventor, "And I can move the earth."

At another time it is said, Archimedes ran bare naked through the streets of his native city, crying "Eureka! Eureka!", which is Greek for "I have found it." The ruler of that city had ordered a goldsmith to make a crown of pure gold and suspecting that the goldsmith had jipped him by dishonestly adding alloy, he handed the crown to Archimedes and asked him to find out if this was so. Archimedes discovered the solution to the problem by observeing the amount of water displaced by his own body while in the process of taking a bath. It was that observation which caused him absentmindedly to run home, with out his cloths, to try the same experiment with the crown.

Archimedes proved that the goldsmith was dishonest. At the same time he proved this principal of the science of Hydrostatics—"That a body imersed in a fluid loses as much in weight as the weight of an equal volume of the fluid."

Not only was Archimedes the greatist mathematician and writer on the science of mechanics among the ancients he was in addition; their greatest inventor. He was one of the greatest scholors of his day.

He was the first to realize the enormous power that can be exerted by means of a lever. He also invented the compound pulley, and a spiral screw for raising water and other substances which is still widely used and is called "Archimede's screw."

When Syracuse, in Sicily (his navive city), was beseiged by the Romans he invented new war engines for it's defense, and suggested a method for using burning glasses to set fire to the beseiging ships. The Romans took the city, but only after a siege of three years and Archimedes was slain in the massacre which followed. It is said that what particularly angered the Roman soldiery was that when they burst in to his house, Archimedes was absorbed in contenplation of mathematical figures which he had drawn on the sand. To the soldier who interupted him, he merely said, "Don't disturb my circles."

Once you have finished editing the text on pages 106 and 107, compare it to our edited version belown. Did you catch all punctuation and spelling errors? Did you notice the same problems our editors did? Were there errors you found that were missed by our editors?

ARCHIMEDES (287-212 B.C.)

"Give me a place to stand and to rest my lever on," said Archimedes the ancient Greek mathematician and inventor, "And I can move the earth."

At another time it is said, Archimedes ran bare naked through the streets of his native city, crying "Eureka! Eureka!" which is Greek for "I have found it." The ruler of that city had ordered a goldsmith to make a crown of pure gold and suspecting that the goldsmith had cheated him by dishonestly adding alloy, he handed the crown to Archimedes and asked him to find out if this was so. Archimedes discovered the solution to the problem by observing the amount of water displaced by his own body while in the process of taking a bath. It was that observation which caused him absentmindedly to run home, with out his cloths, to try the same experiment with the crown.

Archimedes proved that the goldsmith was dishonest. At the same time he proved this principal of principle the science of Hydrostatics—"That a body imersed in a fluid loses as much in weight as the weight of an equal volume of the fluid."

Not only was Archimedes the greatest mathematician and writer on the science of mechanics among the ancients he was in addition their greatest inventor. He was one of the greatest scholars of his day. He was the first to realize the enormous power that can be exerted by means of a lever. He also invented the compound pulley, and a spiral screw for raising water and other substances which is still widely used and is called "Archimede's screw."

When Syracuse, in Sicily (his native city), was beseiged by the Romans he invented new war engines for it's defense, and suggested a method for using burning glasses to set fire to the beseiging ships. The Romans took the city, but only after a siege of three years and Archimedes was slain in the massacre which followed. It is said that what particularly angered the Roman soldiery was that when they burst in to his house, Archimedes was absorbed in contemplation of mathematical figures which he had drawn on the sand. To the soldier who interupted him, he merely said, "Don't disturb my circles."

This was a relatively simple example that did not contain many difficult editing problems. If you had difficulty editing this material, you probably need to get some additional training before attempting to provide copyediting or proofreading services. You do not necessarily need a degree in English (although it is highly recommended). However, your success will depend on your level of skill. Unfortunately, as a publisher, I encounter too many people calling themselves copy editors or proofreaders that do not posses the skill necessary to do an adequate job. Before you start selling your services, make sure you can do a professional job.

TECHNICAL EDITING AND PROOFREADING

The only real difference between technical and general editing and proofreading is that the technical editor/proofreader specializes in a certain field which requires knowledge and understanding of that field, as well as a working vocabulary in that disciple. Law, medicine, geology, physics, chemistry, psychology, and archeology are a few fields where specialized knowledge may be necessary. A technical editor would be useful in editing/proofreading articles written for trade journals and textbooks as well as general interest books in his field. The average editor may not be able to spot a scientific discrepancy or be aware of inconsistencies or new discoveries which would have an impact on the material edited. A thorough knowledge in the field makes the technical editor valuable.

LITERARY CRITIC

How often have you heard someone say, "Someday, I am going to write a book"? Perhaps you may have uttered these words yourself. It seems almost everybody has a secret desire to become a writer. The lure of fame and fortune associated with famous writers instills this desire in many of us. This observation is reinforced by the fact that publishers are bombarded with unsolicited manuscripts from first time authors, most of which are never published.

The primary reason most manuscripts are rejected is they do not meet the standards of publication. Publishers receive so many manuscripts that they can be very choosy. Some are extremely picky and will not even consider material that is not close to perfect. Very few manuscripts are flawless. Most could benefit from an unbiased evaluation or critique. This service is frequently performed by a freelance literary critic.

I've included literary critic services in this chapter because the critic will read and evaluate the client's text, searching, in part, for the same types of errors editors and proofreaders do. Although a critic need not catch every misspelled word, incorrect use of punctuation, poor use of grammar, and other mechanical problems, he or she should make note that such problems exist. The major function of the critic is to critically evaluate the text in terms of the author's writing style and effectiveness in expressing oneself.

Unlike the copy editor and proofreader, the critic will not necessarily make corrections in the text itself. The critic will read the material and write a detailed evaluation for the author, pointing out mechanical errors but focusing on the structural and literary problems. This evaluation should consist of several pages, although comments could be made directly in the text as well.

The purpose of the criticism is to evaluate the text from a literary viewpoint. Most clients will be unpublished writers trying to polish a manuscript they have written. Their ultimate goal is to write well enough to interest book or magazine editors in publishing their material. The critic will point out strengths and weaknesses in the client's work so the author can construct a salable manuscript.

Most unpublished writers who are actively seeking publication of their work do not know how to write well enough to get published. This is one of the main reasons their material is rejected by publishers. They may have some writing talent and be able to write good letters and other materials for personal use, but writing for publication takes a high degree of skill and knowledge. As a publisher myself, I receive many manuscripts and book proposals on topics that have good sales potential, but the authors do not have the literary skills to properly present them. Consequently their material is rejected.

A literary critic can point out problems in a work and help the author improve it and, thus, increase his or her chances on getting it accepted for publication.

A critic looks for many things when evaluating a manuscript. The following are some of the types of questions a critic should answer while reading a client's work. Is the author's writing clear? Would readers understand the descriptions and explanations? This is particularly important with a how-to or self-help type of book. Is the vocabulary consistent and at a level aimed to the readership? A research scientist writing a book for general audiences would lose readers if he used too much scientific terminology. He would need to write for average people without writing down to them in a condescending manner, yet in a way they could understand. Is the material interesting? Does it make the reader want to read more? If it is nonfiction, are the facts and findings presented in an interesting way? Is there supplementary material? This would include maps, charts, graphs, illustrations, appendixes, references, index, footnotes, bibliography, etc. Are they necessary? Are they adequate or incomplete? Are they effectively and properly presented? Do they make a statement or are they there just to fill space?

For fiction and biographies, are the plot and/or subplots clearly defined? Are characters adequately developed? Is suspense or interest maintained throughout the story? Can the author maintain the reader's interest? Does everything make sense? Is the story believable? Are the facts correct or realistic? These are just some of the questions the critic will ask and attempt to answer while reading a manuscript.

How would someone go about learning about what makes good writing? Having a degree in English or literature is highly recommended. Being an English teacher is also an advantage. Part of a teacher's job is to critique students' writing which provides practical experience for such a job. But you don't need to be a teacher or have a degree in literature to work as a freelance literary critic, especially if you have demonstrated your literary skills by being a published author. If you are to help new authors improve their writing so they can get published, you should be a published author yourself. No matter what your background or education, if you have had several books or magazine articles published, you can become a literary critic. If you don't happen to be a published author you can become one. It really isn't as hard as it may seem, as I have described in Chapter 6.

You can increase your skills in this field by taking creative writing classes at your local college or university. Read books on writing technique. Many excellent books are available on different aspects of creative writing and writing in general.

Read good books on any topic. Many famous writers learned their skills from reading the books of other writers and, of course, by writing themselves. They didn't have any formal training, they more or less taught themselves. You can learn a lot about good writing by reading writers' magazines (see the appendix).

ADDITIONAL RESOURCES

I recommend you get as much practice as possible proofreading and copyediting before you start looking for clients. One resource that will help you is *Mark My Words* by Peggy Smith. This book covers the basics of editing and proofreading and contains many practice exercises. The appendix of this book lists several other books and magazines which could help improve your literary skills. There are probably many other good books available at your local library which I have not listed that may also be benificial to you. Read these materials and take classes offered in your community in English, writing, and literature.

You might consider joining a local literary group. Such groups provide support and even potential clients. Often such organizations are listed in the book review section of the newspaper. You may also ask your local librarian if there is a group in your area.

There are two organizations that can be of help to editors and proofreaders. They are the Association of Editorial Businesses and the Editorial Freelancers Association. Write to them for information. See the appendix for the addresses.

CHAPTER 8

BOOK REVIEWING

Books are a valuable resource to many people; they inform, instruct, and entertain. For this reason, newspapers and magazines print reviews of noteworthy books that have recently been published. These reviews are valuable news to many readers and an important part of many publications. In fact, some publications are devoted almost entirely to book reviews.

Book reviewers are also extremely important to book publishers. Book publishers use reviews on their book covers, in catalogs, in advertising, and in other promotional materials. A review provides a unbiased professional opinion on the book, and a good book review can greatly enhance a book's sales. For this reason, publishers actively seek reviews for their titles.

If you like to read, being a book reviewer can open up a fascinating new world for you. You can get access to all the newly published books on the market even before they are available in the local bookstores. You can read works from Stephen King, James Michener, Tom Clancy, and other great writers without ever having to purchase a single book. Reading can be done anywhere and at any time. All you need to do, once you have read the book, is write an evaluation much like a book report.

Book reviewing also opens up the world of journalism to you. As a book reviewer you actually become a freelance reporter—a book reporter. Unlike staff reporters and book editors, as a freelance book reviewer you can work with publications all around the country, often selling reviews of a single book to many of them.

You can take advantage of this marvelous opportunity, but to be successful you need to know how to write usable book reviews and how to sell them. That is what you will learn in this chapter.

HOW TO WRITE BOOK REVIEWS

The purpose of the review is to inform the public of a new book that may be of interest to a certain group of readers. The key word here is *new*. A book review is a news article and therefore should be newsworthy. Newly published books are news. Most reviews are of books that have been out less than one year, although in some cases you may review older books. This is true if you find a book particularly suited for an audience that may not have been adequately exposed to it or a book you have found particularly beneficial or entertaining.

Writing a book review is very similar to writing a short magazine or newspaper article. Book reviews are a form of news reporting. As with all forms of journalism, reviews should be written without prejudice, giving only the merits or deserved criticism and not becoming platforms for expressing personal viewpoints. You mention the good and bad points and, of course, give your opinions, but don't let personal prejudices color your evaluation. The review should be interpretative and explanatory. By making a clear, unbiased evaluation you let readers make their own choice about reading the book.

One very important thing about book reviews is that they are news articles, and as such should be interesting to read and not simply a list of facts about the book and author. Reviews are much like feature news articles. Feature articles are described as detailed presentations of facts in an interesting form for the purpose of entertaining or informing the average reader. Book reviews should do the same.

The reason publications print reviews is because readers like them; if they didn't, reviews wouldn't be printed. There are several reasons people read book reviews: 1) to help them select books that would be of interest; 2) to see what others have to say about a book they have already read; 3) to keep abreast of current literature; and 4) for general interest, reading reviews as they would any other article.

As a reviewer, if you can satisfy the needs of these readers you will have written a good, salable review.

As you see, writing a review involves more than just reading a book and writing a summary or book report. You need to carefully choose the book and read it from the viewpoint of a reviewer. Here are the steps you should take in writing a book review.

Book Selection

What types of books should you choose to review? Many newspapers and other publications primarily print reviews of novels or biographies. *The New York Times* and *The Los Angeles Times*, for example, print almost nothing but this type of material. Magazines will print fiction and nonfiction depending on the type of readership. Trade publications would be mostly interested in nonfiction books in their field of interest. So almost any type of book can conceivably be reviewed, from fiction and nonfiction to cookbooks, poetry, and children's books.

Ask yourself: Does the book have news value? What is it about the book that makes it of interest? If there are a large number of people who would be interested in the book, it has news value.

To some extent, books themselves are news. Old news isn't news, it's history. That is why the majority of reviews are on books which have been on the market less than a year. New novels from well known writers are important to the multitudes of people who anxiously wait for the latest books from their favorite authors. Books on controversial topics and popular trends report on subjects that are currently in the news. Many books create additional news and controversy. Former Iranian leader Ayatollah Khomeini sent shock waves around the world when he put out a death contract on Salman Rushdie, in response to the publication of his novel *The Satanic Verses*. Many books have also been the catalyst for starting new fads and trends. A book that creates news becomes a focus of interest among the public and is an ideal source for a review.

Choose a book that would be of interest to a large number of people. If you will write the review for a newspaper or general interest magazine, the book you choose should be of general interest. If you are writing a review for a trade publication or special interest magazine, your book must be focused to the interests of those readers. A book on antique dolls would be of interest to *Dolls, The Collector's Magazine*, a publication which specializes in dolls, but of little interest to most other periodicals.

Books written by or about celebrities, famous authors, politicians, athletes, and other famous people will be popular whether the books are well written or not. Any book like this, regardless of whether it will become a best seller or not is good for review because readers want to know about the lives and doings of well known people.

Another point to keep in mind when selecting a book for review is to choose a subject you have some background knowledge in or which interests you. If you read a mystery but can't stand mysteries, then your review will suffer and likely be unfairly biased. Likewise, if you read a book on upholstery but don't know anything about it and could care less, your review will likely reflect your attitude. You will do a much better job writing a review of a book about a subject you know and can compare to other works, or one in which you have enthusiasm and interest. You will be more able to write factually and usefully about a subject you are familiar with.

Many trade magazines publish book reviews on a sporadic basis. If you have an interest or experience in a particular subject, you could write a review for a publication which specializes in that particular subject. For example, if you are a stamp collector, you could review a book for *Stamp Collector* magazine. For a publication such as *Calligraphy Review,* you would review calligraphy books; for *World Tennis* you would review books on tennis or about tennis players. Be very specific. Don't send *Opera News* a review on a book about a great violinist, unless the violinist was somehow actively involved in opera. There are hundreds of special interest magazines and trade journals for which you could write reviews. You would probably have better luck selling a review to these types of magazines because you would be reviewing a specific type of book and will probably have less competition from other reviewers.

Most publications you will probably be interested in are general interest magazines and newspapers. These publications aren't generally interested in any specific type of subject but publish reviews that will be of most interest to most of their readers. These would be general interest books, particularly fiction books such as novels, but nonfiction books as well. Some publications will only print reviews of novels, while others will print most anything they believe would interest their readers.

Many general interest books will interest a large number of publications. Books on popular subjects and trends, and books by famous authors or by or about celebrities all have wide appeal and could be sold to a number of publications. Some books will have a strong appeal to certain readers and publications, but not for most others. For instance, a book on cactus gardens would be most appropriate for publications located in the Southwest and other dry climates in the United States. A newspaper in Pennsylvania would have little interest in publishing a review of such a book. This example may have been obvious, but there are many topics which may not be. Another example would be a book about the oil industry. People in Alaska, California, Oklahoma, Texas, and Louisiana would be interested in this book because of the large oil industry in these states which has a pronounced effect on many of their lives and economies. Most people in Maine would have little interest because there is no oil industry there to speak of. A book on sailing would interest people who

live near large bodies of water. If you choose your book carefully and zero in on publications whose readers would be most
interested in the subject, you will have success.

Read

Your next step is to read the book. When you read it, read it,
don't just skim through. Many book editors and staff reviewers
must read rapidly in order to get through the myriad of books
that are sent to them. Often they cannot read the book in detail,
but rely on publishers' comments, book descriptions, and previous reviews for much of their information. As a freelance book
reviewer, however, you are expected to thoroughly read each
book you review. So take your time and read at a comfortable
pace.

Take Notes

As you read the book, take notes. Make note of the book's good
and bad points as you go along. Don't trust everything to
memory. The more detailed notes you take the easier it will be
to write the review.

You should also select quotations that you can use in your
review. Select interesting passages that reflect the scope and
focus of the book. For humorous books such as those written by
Erma Bombeck and Bill Cosby, for example, you could choose
some particularly funny comments which illustrate the quality
and tone of the book.

For a book of fiction, you should take notes on the plot and
how it is developed, the setting, the characters, and the author's
writing style. For a nonfiction book, here are some samples of
the types of questions you could ask yourself:

- What is the approach or point of view of the author?
- Is the author qualified to write such a book?
- How is the subject matter organized?
- What source material was used in preparing the book?
- Are instructions clear and detailed?
- Are the facts and information in the book accurate?

- Who is the book written for (youth or adult; men or women; professional, hobbyist, or casual reader, etc.)?
- Will the book be out of date soon or will it be useful for many years?
- Are any important new facts or perspectives presented?
- Are illustrations, photos, graphs, maps appendix, and other supporting information effectively presented and used?

For a novel, you would take notes on the plot development, main characters, writing style, and how well the book holds your interest.

Choose an Angle

When you select a book to read, you need to know from the start what type of audience it is intended for and what publications these people read. With this in mind, as you read you will decide on an appropriate angle or theme in which to present the review. The theme should reflect the readers' interests. Many books themselves incorporate a theme or expresses a strong viewpoint which you can use to develop the focus of your review.

Let me give you an example. A book on walking for exercise and health, which may be written and enjoyable for readers of any age, could have a strong emphasis toward senior citizens. If you are writing a review for a publication that is primarily for senior citizens, you should focus on this aspect of the book. If the review is for a woman's publication, you would focus on the benefits women can gain from the book. Make your review of interest to the reader.

Outline

Once you have read the book, use your notes to write an outline incorporating your chosen theme. Don't neglect this step, it will help you organize your thoughts in a coherent effective manner and save you time when you write the review.

Write the Review

The next step is simply to write the review. Keep in mind that the best reviews are interesting news articles and not just a rehash of the book's contents. Most good reviews will cover these points:

• Description of the contents of the book.
• Some information about the author.
• A comparison of the book to others by the same author or of the same genre.
• Evaluation of the goal or purpose of the book.
• Description of what the book has to offer the reader.
• A judgment of the book's quality and usefulness.

When reviewing a book on fiction one rule to keep in mind is do not divulge too much of the plot and, by all means, do not give away the ending to the story! Do not remove the surprise and enjoyment for readers. People read fiction to be amused or entertained; that impact of the book can be destroyed by revealing the ending. Focus your comments on the setting, characters, writing style, and only briefly cover the plot. Give just enough to make it interesting to readers and give them a general idea about the type of book it is. Express your opinion about the story in general and the author's skill in presenting it.

Keep in mind as you write the review that you are not supposed to make up the reader's mind. Reviews are supposed to help readers make up their own minds as to whether a book is for them or not.

Edit and Rewrite
After finishing your first draft of the review, go through it again and polish it. Correct spelling and grammatical errors. Go over your review several times and make your thoughts and choice of words flow smoothly. After you are finished with the rewriting, set the review aside without looking at it for a few days, and longer if possible. After this time review and reread it. You will probably be surprised at how many changes you will think are necessary. Rewrite it again. The reason for setting the review aside is that writers in general get so attached to their work that sometimes they cannot see the errors or inadequacies it contains.

The material looks good to the author because it is still fresh in his or her mind, and there may be some emotional attachment. After waiting for a period of time, the author can look at the work more objectively and catch errors that weren't apparent before.

Prepare and Submit the Review

The finished review should be double-spaced and type-written on only one side of the paper. You should follow the manuscript format described in Chapter 6 for submitting articles. After all, a book review is a special feature article. Unlike typical newspaper and magazine articles, a book review will also contain an *indicia*. The indicia is a listing of the book title, author, publisher, and price. It may also contain some additional information such as place of publication, publisher's address, ISBN number, number of pages, and indicate if index, bibliography, and illustrations are included. This information is compressed into a single paragraph and is usually in the form of a series of short phrases, as in this example:

Writing Effective News Releases by Catherine V. McIntyre. Piccadilly Books, P.O. Box 25203, Colorado Springs, CO 80936. $16.95.

A more detailed indicia would look like the following:

Writing Effective News Releases by Catherine V. McIntyre. Piccadilly Books, P.O. Box 25203, Colorado Springs, CO 80936. 176 pp. Paper, $16.95 (ISBN 0-941599-19-1). Photographs; illustrations; appendices. 8-1/2" x 11".

The indicia is usually listed at the beginning of the review, but is also often placed at the end. In feature articles on books it is usually somewhere in the body of the text. Follow the format of the publication you submit your review to.

One of the best ways to learn how to write good book reviews is to read and study good book reviews. Read the reviews printed in *The New York Times*, *The Los Angeles Times*,

The Chicago Tribune, and other papers. Most libraries subscribe to these papers so they should be available to you. Familiarity with their style and format will help prepare you to write your own reviews. Analyze how they grab reader's attention; what are the articles' slant or theme; and what are the pros and cons of the books; what reasons do the reviewers give for their conclusions?

HOW TO MARKET YOUR REVIEWS

Book reviews are sold much the same way magazine articles are. Perhaps the biggest difference is that rather than send a query letter to the publication you would send the entire review. There are a couple of reasons for this. Book reviews are very short and it takes just about as much time to read one as it does to read a query letter. Another reason is that most of the reviews you send will be to newspapers rather than magazines, and newspapers usually expect to receive the completed material.

Submit your review to the book editor or if the paper doesn't have a book editor, the city editor or to the publisher or managing editor for a magazine. Address your letter to the editor by name rather than just using a title. Use the same type of format you would for a magazine article as described in Chapter 6. Include a cover letter briefly describing your review and your qualifications. This should be no more than a few paragraphs.

Most book editors have a list of reviewers they rely on for the majority of their reviews. These reviewers consist of staff members, freelancers, and specialists in various fields. If you can supply interesting reviews that meet the requirements of the editor, he will probably add your name to the list.

Your hardest job will be breaking in with a new publication. Once a magazine or newspaper has accepted a review from you, additional reviews will be easier to sell to them. They will know who you are and you build a working relationship.

Look in *Literary Market Place* and *Writer's Market* for newspapers and magazines which print or accept book reviews. *Literary Market Place* contains an up to date listing of all newspapers in the country. Listings for the major newspapers also include the names of the editors of each department, so that you can find the book review editor. It also contains a listing of newspapers which print book reviews, as many do not. *Writer's Market* contains a detailed listing of magazines, some of which buy book reviews. You can uncover those publications which do by searching through the magazine and trade journal sections.

Keep track of all publications which publish reviews and send a query to see if they buy freelance book reviews. Include a self-addressed stamped envelope for a reply. Even better than an envelope would be a self-addressed stamped postcard. Type or print something like this on one side:

Please answer the questions below and return.
Do you accept freelance book reviews? ___Yes, ___No.
Do you currently have a need for reviews from freelance book reviewers? ___Yes, ___No.
What types of books are you most interested in at the present?_____
Comments_____
_____

Editors are very busy people. Providing them with a post-card that can be checked off easily will lessen their work load and more likely get you a reply.

Record your results by making two lists. One list will consist of all those who accept freelance book reviews and indicate a need for reviews. The second list will be of those publications which buy reviews, but are not currently looking for submissions from additional book reviewers. Your primary list will be those who are willing to accept your reviews. Submit your reviews to these publications first. But do not ignore the other publications that publish freelance reviews but are not currently looking for new reviewers. Many of them will still buy your reviews. They indicated no current need for them because they are probably already working with several people who supply them with useful reviews. That doesn't mean they won't buy a review from you if it fits their needs. You can still sell to them, although competition may make it a little harder.

HOW TO GET BOOKS FOR REVIEW

As a book reviewer, you have a special opportunity not available to most people and that is to receive and read books free of charge. Publishers set aside a certain number of their newly published books to give to reviewers. Usually books are sent routinely to only a handful of select reviewers, publications, and news syndicates. Everyone else is sent news releases and flyers. After all, the books are the publishers' products and publishers cannot afford to send free copies to every reviewer or book editor in the country. If, after receiving publicity material from the publisher, reviewers are interested in reviewing the book, they can request a review copy be sent to them.

You can request a review copy of a book from the publisher. Most publishers, in hopes of getting a book review, will send a free copy of the book to any reviewer who requests it. Some publishers may require some sort of verification that you are a bona fide reviewer. They don't want to send free books to just anyone who asks or who claims to be a reviewer. You should always make your requests on your business letterhead and stationery. This will show the publisher you are a professional reviewer and not just someone trying to gather free books. Your letterhead could read something like: "Joan Callihan, Freelance Reviewer." Another way to verify yourself is to include copies of a few of your reviews which were published. Write on the top of the review the name and date of publication.

You can offer to buy the book, but if publishers know it is for review purposes they will frequently give it to you free. Sometimes skeptical publishers may still require payment. Most free review copies will be stamped "Review Copy" or "Not For Resale" so you cannot sell them to used bookstores.

You can request book catalogs from publishers. Have the publishers put your name on their mailing lists so you are informed of all the new titles coming out. They will be glad to do this for legitimate reviewers.

It is important you collect and save copies of any reviews you get published. You will use these clippings to show publishers you are a legitimate reviewer so they will send you review copies of their books. You can also send book editors copies of your reviews to convince them that you are a professional reviewer and they could benefit from your services. *You should always send the publisher a copy of any published review.* This is true even if the book review editor is the one who gave the book to you. This is done out of courtesy to the publisher, and let's him know the book he sent (to you or the editor) was used. He will then be more inclined to send additional books in the future. I would like to stress the importance of sending the publisher clippings. Publishers want to know if reviews of their books have been printed. They have no way of knowing unless the reviewer notifies them. Publishers use reviews in their publicity and marketing efforts, and that is one of the primary reasons they are willing to give out free copies of their books. Thank them by sending the clippings.

Another way you can find books to review is by reading book review magazines. The major review magazines are *Booklist, Kirkus Reviews, Library Journal,* and *Publishers Weekly.* These magazines are used by librarians, bookstores, distributors, schools, and others in the book trade to find out about potentially popular new books. These reviewers print their reviews at about the same time the books are published and released to the public; for this reason they are also referred to as prepublication reviewers. Publishers send them sample copies of their books before they go to press, and frequently, if the review comes out before publication, they can use the reviews on the book covers. You should become familiar with these publications and with many of the other book review magazines that are published. Libraries usually have subscriptions to these magazines and you can read them there.

These publications only review books they believe are good and will become popular. They publish probably only one review for every ten books they receive. Generally, a review is a recommendation to readers to buy the book. You can find many potential books for you to read from these sources. You will have a printed review available to judge the contents, and know who the publisher is so you can obtain your own review copy. Although this will give you many potential books to review, don't neglect the books that were not reviewed by these publications. You can sell many reviews on good books passed over by these reviewers and that is another reason you want to request that publishers put you on their mailing list.

Each spring and fall, *Publishers Weekly* lists the best new books from publishers. These are books that will be published in the coming months which publishers feel will be their best new titles. You should make it a point to read these issues each year and choose likely review candidates.

You can also find new books in the library. Often a library will put new acquisitions on a separate shelf for a few months before mixing them into the rest of their collections. By browsing through these books you may find some excellent books for review that you had not found elsewhere. The name and address of the publisher will usually be found on the copyright page, which is just behind the title page. If a complete address is not there, you can look up the publisher's address in *Writer's Market* or *Books in Print*, both of which are available at your local library.

As I mentioned, most of the book reviews in prepublication book review sources are generally positive. And most book reviews in general are positive. Usually a poor or mediocre book will not be reviewed. There are just too many good books available and too little space to waste it on second-rate or inappropriate books. For this reason, you should concentrate on good books or books that will have some significant impact. Some books, because they are written by a famous author or celebrity or are about a popular celebrity or new trend, are important to review even though they may not be particularly good books. This would be the only time you would write an unpraiseworthy review. Be honest in any review you write—

state the good points and the bad. If the book doesn't deserve a good review, don't review it unless it is one many people would buy because of the popularity of the author or subject matter. Publishers will frequently send a sample book review or news release describing the book along with the review copy. News releases and sample reviews can help busy newspaper editors or reviewers write their reviews. They can use the information as a basis for their reviews. In some cases news releases and sample reviews are reprinted almost word-for-word, or with just minor editing. Many news releases and sample reviews are too commercial to be reprinted as is, but they are good in bringing out highlights of the book. Freelance reviewers should write their own reviews. Don't ruin your reputation by copying the publisher's review. After all, the publisher may have sent the newspaper editor the same material he sent to you.

ADDITIONAL INFORMATION

For additional information that would help you improve your skills as a book reviewer, I recommend you read books on journalism, book reviewing, writing book reports, and magazines for writers (see appendix for resources). There are many good book review publications I have not mentioned. Reading them will also improve your reviewing skills and give you leads for books to review for other publications. Ask your librarian for a list of review publications.

CHAPTER 9

RESEARCHING

Do you like to read crime and mystery novels? Are you one of those people who find news reports and true life mysteries fascinating? Do you mentally try to fit the pieces together to solve the mystery yourself? Are you intrigued by trivia and other little known facts of science, history, geography, and politics? If so, you may enjoy being a researcher.

Researchers are much like detectives. They search for clues to solve mysteries. The mystery, in this case, is to locate information. In fact, many private investigators use the researcher's methods to locate information for their clients.

Many businesses and individuals use researchers to search out and find information for them. The information they locate is not necessarily hidden or unknown. In fact, most of the information a researcher is asked to find is readily accessible in the library and available to anyone who wants it. The problem is most people do not know where or how to look for it. Learning how to become a researcher really only involves learning what types of resources and services are available in the library and knowing how to use them.

Magazine publishers routinely use researchers or fact checkers to verify facts in newly written articles before they are published. The credibility of the magazine depends on reporting and writing accurately so they hire fact checkers to confirm the accuracy of authors' statements. If an author claims back pain is the second most common reason given for missing work by people over the age of 40, a researcher might look it up for verification. If an author states that boxer John L. Sullivan had a professional boxing record of 58 wins and 10 losses, the facts may need to be checked. Most fact checking, however, is to varify dates and the spelling of names.

Businesses frequently need researchers to find information on current economic trends, uncover information about their competitors, identify consumer tastes, or find geographic, ethnic, and cultural preferences to effectively market and promote their products or services. The types of questions may include: What is the population of people over 55 years of age in the state of Vermont? What percentage of home buyers with incomes over $100,000 per year use FHA guaranteed loans? What are the ages, income levels, marital status, and family sizes of the majority of people who subscribe to *Sports Illustrated* magazine? This last question could be very valuable to a company interested in purchasing advertising space in the magazine. Before they make the investment, they would want to know if the readers are the type who would purchase their products.

Writers are also a major source for researcher services. In writing books and articles, they need to find facts about their subjects. Many questions could simply entail locating facts or statistics; others could involve more comprehensive material and involve writing a report or summary of your findings. You may be asked to learn the history behind a house that current owners claim is haunted. Another client may want you to find the number of cases reported annually of police brutality in the state of California and what percentage goes to court. Another may want to know the ingredients of B & M External Remedy, a fraudulent ointment used to treat cuts and abrasions in the 1930s. By the way, the answer to this last question is turpentine,

ammonia, and eggs. This information was found in a book titled
*100,000,000 Guinea Pigs: Dangers in Everyday Foods, Drugs,
and Cosmetics.* Many people also use researchers to find their roots. Some
people who may not know their parents want to find out about
them, while others want to trace their lineage back into history
as far as possible. So some researchers become very skilled at
doing genealogical research.

Although finding the information I have mentioned in the
previous paragraphs may sound insurmountable to you at this
time, much of it is readily available in libraries. If you know
where to look, it is surprisingly easy to find. It might take five
minutes to get what you need, or it might take hours, depending
of the type of information and your knowledge of the available
resources. Even if the library does not contain the facts you are
seeking, it can lead you to a source that does. If you're lucky,
you will be able to go to a single source to look up the needed
information. But frequently, you will need to search through
many resources, picking up clues that will eventually lead to a
source with the correct answer. These facts could be located in
reference books or directories, textbooks, general interest books,
magazines, newsletters, reports, pamphlets, microfilm, video or
audio cassettes, and at times, even knowledgeable people.

TYPES OF LIBRARIES

Libraries contain more than just books for casual reading. They
are storehouses of information of all sorts. Most people do not
realize the enormous amount and wide variety of information
available at their local library. With the use of interlibrary loan,
where materials can be obtained from other libraries, almost any
type of information is obtainable, regardless of where you live.

There are different types of libraries you should become
familiar with. Each contains different collections. No two libraries are exactly alike. And obviously, the larger the library, the
more resources it will have available.

Public Libraries

These libraries contain books to serve the general public. These collections consist of recreational and informational books on a variety of topics of interest to children, adults, crafts people, hobbyists, etc. They have many popular literary titles for those who enjoy reading for pleasure, as well as nonfiction and instructional texts for those seeking understanding in various fields.

Large public libraries have extensive resources and reference books that allow you to find information on just about anything.

Academic Libraries

College and university libraries cater to the needs of scholars, students, and researchers and will have a more complete collection of specialized and technical materials than a public library would. Most of the materials are on a scholarly or professional level not found in public libraries.

College libraries collect materials in the academic fields taught at the school. Some universities have special strengths or offer programs not available at most other schools, such as dentistry, law, or film-making. They would have extensive collections on these subjects in their libraries.

Generally, you should use the largest library at your disposal. Frequently, this would be your local academic library and not the public library. Besides having a larger volume of materials, university libraries generally have a more complete selection of directories, indexes, and other tools that identify resources which will help you in your research.

You don't have to be a student or faculty member to use these libraries. Anyone can use the resources; however, if you plan on checking out any materials or requisitioning any special library services, you will need to get a library card. The general public can get library cards for an annual fee which ranges from $10 to $50. This will allow you the same privileges as students and faculty members.

Historical Society and Museum Libraries

Historical society collections and museum libraries are usually subject-oriented. Historical societies and museums are built around a theme or cover a certain period of history. The subject could be general such as the Civil War or natural history, or very specific such as to honor the memory of a single person, place, or even a building. These library collections would be devoted entirely to these subjects. Books that may not easily be found in other libraries may find a home here.

These organizations may own documents available nowhere else such as diaries, historical records, membership rolls, and such, all of which could be of use to a researcher. Also, the curators or society members are often specialists in their field and could be a valuable source of information.

If a researcher is looking for information on a topic for which there is a museum or historical society, these would be the most likely places to look. If the library does not have the information sought, the librarian may know the answer or know someone who would.

Private and Special Libraries

Other collections that may be of help to a researcher are company, newspaper, hospital, federal, state, consulate, embassy, church, association, and chamber of commerce libraries and resources. Many of these organizations maintain libraries for the use of their members or employees. Sometimes the public is restricted, but most will allow researchers to use their facilities.

Some of these special libraries may be the only place where certain data may be found. Most churches, for example, contain information such as baptismal and marriage records from which genealogies can be derived. Some churches maintain extensive genealogical collections that can be found nowhere else. The data they have are compiled from public, private, and church records from around the world and extend back hundreds of years.

Businesses also can be a resource. If you wanted to learn about the personal life of Frank Phillips, the founder of Phillips Petroleum Company, the best place to look is in one of the Phillips Petroleum Company's libraries. The company maintains libraries in most all of their regional offices as well as their headquarters in Bartlesville, Oklahoma, which would have the most extensive collection of information.

RESEARCH TOOLS

The number of resource books and materials available is staggering and I cannot begin to cover them all here. I will, however, mention some of the most useful resources you will use in your research. This will give you an idea of what types of materials are available and what materials a researcher is expected to know how to use.

Books

The most obvious resources for information in libraries are books. By looking up the subject of interest in the card catalog, which nowadays is most often accessed through a computer terminal, you may locate books which might hold the information sought. This is often one of the first methods used by people who use the library, but it is one of the slowest processes in getting facts. If all you need is to check facts, find statistics, or locate a bit of obscure information, your best source would not be here but with reference books and directories.

Books are more helpful for detailed or extensive research, or if other resources cannot be found. For example, it would be much easier and quicker to look up George Custer's birthplace in an encyclopedia than in a biography of the man. However, if you want to find some detailed information about Custer's personal life before he entered the military, a biography may be more appropriate.

Magazines and Newspapers

To find current information the best place to look is in magazines and newspapers. Through these sources we find out what is new in the world and in all aspects of life from finance to parenting. Trade journals and association newsletters publish research and studies of interest to select audiences and professions. It is in these periodicals that a researcher may find information contained nowhere else. There are thousands of magazines, newsletters, and trade journals, all of which are written for a specific type of audience. Subject matter of these publications varies from horse racing *(The Quarter Horse Journal)* to stamp collecting *(Stamp Collector)*.

Most libraries have subscriptions to several periodicals, including local newspapers. Magazines are collected over a period of time, then bound and put on the shelves. Back issues of newspapers are stored on microform. Some libraries do not allow patrons to check out periodicals, so you would have to read them in the library. If the library does not have the issue of the magazine or newspaper you need, they can get a copy of the article you want through interlibrary loan. Through the interlibrary loan system, you have access to current and past issues of virtually every major newspaper and magazine in the country. A most valuable resource to researchers.

Reference Books

Reference books are storehouses of information. They include encyclopedias, dictionaries, almanacs, chronologies, handbooks, and yearbooks. They are good sources for information, but not the only source or even the best source.

Everyone is familiar with the general reference books such as *Webster's Dictionary* and the *Encyclopedia Americana.* These general resources are the first place most everybody goes for information, but there are hundreds more. Yes, hundreds! Most people are unaware these references even exist. Unlike the general references most people know about, these reference books focus on select themes or topics. For example, there are dictionaries for medicine, engineering, geology, psychology, and foreign languages, as well as historical dictionaries, thesauruses, dictionaries of slang, rhyming dictionaries, and many others. Encyclopedias are even more numerous and varied. There are encyclopedias of science, history, literature, religion, social sciences, education, music, psychology, philosophy, and art. These may consist of a single volume or be sets containing 30 or more books.

Almanacs are excellent sources for miscellaneous facts. These annual references contain some information on almost everything, including statistics on things like sports, population, births and deaths, price and production rates, names of government officials, and information on the states and all countries of the world. Like dictionaries and encyclopedias, there are many different types of almanacs.

These and other reference books contain information on just about anything you can imagine. Information on people, history, science, politics, culture, recreation, entertainment, arts, religion, geography, literature, and more are covered in handbooks, chronologies, yearbooks, gazetteers, and other reference books.

Directories and Indexes

Directories and indexes are books of lists. For directories, the lists could be phone numbers, addresses, personal or company names, etc. The phone book is one example. Other directories list associations, manufacturers, corporations, theme parks, famous people, newspapers, magazines, and books.

One important directory you should become familiar with is *Subject Guide to Books in Print*. It lists, by subject, every book currently in print. If you need information on a particular subject, you can look in this directory to see if there are any books available. You don't need to know the name of the author or the book because all books are listed by subject.

Indexes are invaluable to the serious researcher. They may not contain facts themselves, but they tell where to go to find information you may be seeking. If you are looking for current information on divorce, for example, and remember seeing a magazine article about it a few months ago but can't remember which one, you could look in *Reader's Guide to Periodical Literature*. This index lists the article title, date, and name of the publication for all articles published in about 160 popular magazines. By looking up the subject you will not only find the magazine article you were looking for, but every article written on divorce published in these magazines. The index contains many volumes and goes as far back as 1900.

Reader's Guide to Periodical Literature is the best known and most used index, but there are many others which focus on publications with specific interests. Some of the specialized topics covered by other indexes are agriculture, art, business, education, music, and science. Besides magazine articles, some indexes list book and film reviews, poems, plays, songs, speeches, and other pieces of information. Many newspapers compile indexes which list references to all of their articles.

Government Documents

A government document is a publication issued through the authority of a government agency. The United States government is the largest publisher in North America. Hundreds of government agencies, bureaus, offices, executive departments, and regulatory agencies devote a great deal of their time and resources to producing studies and reports for publication. These materials include documents, brochures, pamphlets, dictionaries, directories, catalogs, indexes, atlases, magazines, and books covering a wide variety of subjects, ranging from in-depth demographic studies to parenting, gardening, and health advice.

Government publications are often the most up-to-date and authoritative material available. Government agencies research, gather and analyze statistics, and compile their findings on a regular basis, so you can have access to the latest studies and research.

Most libraries do not handle government publications as they do other materials. They are cataloged using a different numbering system and placed in their own section of the library with a separate catalog. Although some documents are included in commercially published indexes, the majority are found in specific indexes such as Monthly Catalog and CIS/Index and Abstracts to Publications of the U.S. Congress. Because government publications are separated and cataloged differently from other collections in the library, most people are unaware they even exist. It is worth your time to become familiar with the many valuable government resources in your local library.

Personal Computers

With the growing popularity of personal computers and computer services, much of the research you do can be done at home. If you have a personal computer and a modem, you can access library information as well as use data from private information services.

You have access to a wealth of information with a computer information service. Material that is available include theater and book reviews, current news, complete magazine and newspaper articles, business reports, horoscopes, encyclopedias, indexes, weather forecasts, soap opera updates, and Nielsen ratings, as well as information about financial planning, sports, arts, environment, education, travel, and health. The list can go on and on.

Of course, there are fees required for using these services. The cost can vary greatly from a monthly charge of only a few dollars, regardless of how often you use the service, up to several dollars per minute of computer access time. The cost depends on the company and the information used.

There are hundreds of private computer information services. Perhaps the four most popular and useful are CompuServe, Dow Jones News Retrieval, The Knowledge Index, and Prodigy. Addresses for these services are included in the appendix. Write to them for further information. To find out about other companies and about the computer services offered by your local library ask your librarian.

ADDITIONAL RESOURCES

I have kept my description of library resources very brief, just to give you a feel for the types of materials you would need to know about as a researcher. There are hundreds of additional resources available. With proper preparation, you can learn on your own, everything you need to know in order to become a good researcher. Go to your local library and learn as much about it as you can. Practice using the microfiche machines. Browse through the reference books to get a feel for the types of resources available. The biggest hurdle in finding facts is knowing where to look. If you become very familiar with the references in the library, you can save time by automatically going to the most likely source.

I recommend, if possible, that you take some classes in library science at your local college or university. That would be the best way to learn what you need to know. If these types of classes are not available in your area, you can take a correspondence course from a number of universities with library science programs. You can locate the names and addresses of appropriate schools at your local library. It should have school catalogs, or at least microfiche of the catalogs, for you to examine. The librarian will be able to help you find appropriate schools.

Whether you take classes or learn on your own, the only way you can become a good researcher is by practice. Ask yourself some obscure questions and see how well you can do in finding the answers. As you practice, you will learn how to use the reference materials and get a feel for what information is located where.

When you are first trying to learn about the library's resources, you can always ask the reference librarian for help. If you get stuck trying to locate some information, the library staff will be more than happy to assist you, so long as you don't monopolize their time. They are willing to spend a few minutes helping library patrons. Usually they will point out some possible reference sources and allow you to search through the pages for the needed information yourself. Use them when needed but don't depend entirely on them.

To learn about these resources and how libraries work, you should read and study some of the books on researching and library science located in the library. I highly recommend the book *Knowing Where to Look: The Ultimate Guide to Research* by Lois Horowitz. This book is very easy to read and extremely interesting. It will give you everything you need to know to start off as a researcher.

CHAPTER 10

TRANSLATING

Can you read and write a foreign language? If you can, you may have the skills that will open the door to a wonderful career as a freelance translator. Opportunities for translation services are available throughout the country and are in high demand.

Translating, essentially is reading material in one language and rewriting it in another. Ordinarily, translators translate writing of a foreign language into their native tongue. If you can read and understand a foreign language, then you can translate. Rarely do translators convert their native language into a foreign one.

Translating provides a unique reading opportunity in a wide variety of subject areas. If you like the thrill and intrigue of being a part of international politics and current events, you could work for the CIA or FBI. If you prefer reading literary works such as novels, short stories, and poetry, then translating for publishing companies would fit your interests. If you have skills or even just interests in medicine, engineering, economics, finance, science, social services, or other subjects you can find businesses, private organizations, and government agencies which need translators.

The three main categories of materials most frequently translated are commercial, literary, and technical. The first includes business correspondence, product descriptions and instructions, contracts, and advertising literature. The second involves working with books, articles, music lyrics, and other literary works. The third, technical translating, comprises material in the various sciences and engineering.

Many businesses and organizations primarily need general translating services. Some, however, require the translator to have background knowledge in a certain industry or subject area to be able to translate competently. In fact, background knowledge makes the translator much more valuable. Literary translators need to possess good writing skills comparable to that of the author in order to convey the emotional and artistic as well as the informational content of the original. The language should be normal and natural so the reader is unaware the material is a translation. Knowledge of finance may be necessary to properly translate a company's annual financial reports. Or a knowledge of medicine in order to properly translate a medical text. That does not mean the translator needs to be an expert in the field or even have any formal training in it. Many translators pick up the specialized terminology and knowledge of the business or industry from practice and personal research.

Events over the past several years have brought about changes in the way people work and interact with each other, both within the country and from one country to another. Foreign trade, political and social interaction, and travel have greatly increased, creating many exciting opportunities for people who have foreign language skills.

COMMERCE AND BUSINESS

Our planet is shrinking. New technology links the world as never before. Countries around the globe are only seconds away by fax, phone, or satellite link. Because of advances in technology, doing business overseas is not the barrier it once was.

Today American businesses are worldwide. American products such as blue jeans, almonds, and videos are sold throughout the world. Likewise, thousands of foreign companies export goods into our country. All you need to do is look at your local stores and see the prevalence of French and Italian clothes, and Japanese radios, television sets, and automobiles. Foreign made products abound.

Because of the restrictive import laws of some countries, it has become necessary for American companies to establish branch offices and manufacturing plants in many host countries in order to effectively reach new markets. This often requires going into a partnership with a company in the host country or with the government itself. Thousands of U.S. companies have foreign operations and connections.

What this indicates is there is and will continue to be a tremendous need and opportunity for translation services. Even though companies may have employees who can speak, read, and write foreign languages, these people are frequently too busy with other responsibilities to take the time to translate technical information, product descriptions, advertisements, brochures, correspondence, and documents. Freelance translators are routinely used for this purpose.

Even though a company may not actively market goods outside this country, it still may need translation services occasionally. At my book publishing company we do not seek publishing rights to foreign books or manuscripts, nor do we actively market our books overseas. However, we do receive inquiries from booksellers, customers, and authors overseas quite frequently, and must deal with correspondence in foreign languages.

There are many types of businesses that, just by their nature, need the services of translators. Some of these organizations which readily come to mind include travel agencies, import-export businesses, publishers, advertising agencies, hotels, tourist attractions, attorneys, and nonprofit organizations.

The travel industry, for example, holds great potential for language services. Over 20 million tourists visit the United

States every year. Tour operators in foreign countries stress the need for more tour and travel literature in their languages. Translators are necessary for preparing promotional materials and giving assistance to travel agents, hotels, restaurants, tour companies, and the like.

Businesses and organizations do not necessarily need to be involved in foreign trade to need translation services. Simply doing business in this country can require foreign language services. America is a melting pot of people from countries all around the world who speak many different languages. Frequently, immigrants have not mastered English before coming to this country. Many settle in communities dominated by people who speak their native languages. Consequently, many of these immigrants never really learn how to speak English. Currently, there are over 25 million foreign born people living in the United States. The six most often spoken languages, in order, are Spanish, Italian, German, French, Polish, and Chinese.

Businesses who hire non-English speaking people must have access to bilingual personnel capable enough to translate company policies, insurance information, benefits, and such. Many businesses, in an effort to reach new markets for their goods, focus advertising toward these people, translating advertising literature and product descriptions into their language. Some businesses, such as legal services, are needed by all residents and must use translators to translate legal documents. Lawyers handle business transactions, divorces, and other lawsuits, as well as help obtain visas and process citizenship papers for immigrants. In order to reach these people, businesses must become bilingual.

GOVERNMENT

Over the past several decades the United States has emerged as an economic, social, and political world leader. It hosts the United Nations and has foreign offices and military installations in hundreds of foreign countries. Because of the dominant position of the United States in world affairs and the need for effective communication, a great demand exists for people with foreign language training. In Europe, because of economic and social pressure, the learning of foreign languages has been a requirement. In America, however, the need to learn a second language has not been considered a necessity. Foreign language training has not been emphasized and consequently most Americans are not bilingual. The great need for and lack of qualified people has created many opportunities for those who do possess foreign language skills.

The federal government is the largest employer of translators. The Department of State needs translators in dozens of foreign languages and employs both full and part-time foreign language specialists, most of whom are freelancers. The Division of Language Services is responsible for all official translations for the Department of State. This includes translating from foreign languages into English, and from English into foreign languages.

The Joint Publications Research Service (JPRS), an agency of the CIA, is one of the largest employers of freelance translators. They work on a large number of articles on social, political, and economic topics translated for use by the government.

Translators are, in general, asked to translate into their native language. A translator must be able to write his or her native language with a high degree of skill. Those who translate English into foreign languages must be able to write in those languages with all the skill of a professional writer native to the language, since most translations are intended for distribution abroad. Material translated includes newspapers, magazines, scientific/technical journals, manuals, maps, and   transcripts of foreign radio broadcasts.

For further information about working as a freelance translator with the federal government contact the following offices:

U.S. Department of State
Office of Foreign Languages, Rm 2212
200 C St. N.W.
Washington, D.C. 20520

U.S. JPRS
1000 North Glebe Road
Arlington, VA 22201

Federal Bureau of Investigation
Department of Justice
Washington, D.C. 20535

U.S. Information Agency
301 Fourth St, S.W.
Washington, D.C. 20451

Both federal and local governments, as well as private social services, actively need and use people with foreign language skills. Social services help people who have difficulty dealing with problems in life. Services include child welfare, mental, spiritual, and physical health, education, etc. People in need could either be residents of this country or another. Government and nonprofit groups work here and abroad to provide needed help.

Some of the nonprofit organizations that provide services include the Peace Corps, Red Cross, and YMCA. Many religious groups are also involved in foreign affairs. They need hymns, tracts, and other literature translated for their missionary and humanitarian efforts.

LITERARY TRANSLATING

Although literary translating may be performed for government, business, and other organizations, it is usually associated with the publishing and film industries. Literary translation is different from commercial and technical translation because it requires a higher degree of creative writing talent. Literary translators almost always convert material from a foreign language into their native tongue. The value of the translation is dependent on the translator's ability with his or her mother language.

Publishers and film production companies frequently hire freelance translators to convert foreign language books and manuscripts into English. Publishers need translations of poetry, short stories, novels, textbooks, articles, technical manuals, and other materials. Production companies look for books and scripts that could be adapted to television, motion pictures, or plays.

Book publishers are constantly seeking manuscripts written by foreign authors or books which have been published abroad. They receive books and manuscripts from authors, agents, and publishers from other countries to consider for publication here.

Even though the publisher may have qualified editors who can read and translate the material, these people are too busy to do it themselves. Few publishing houses employ in-house translators, so translators are usually hired on a freelance basis for each project.

If a manuscript or book is accepted for publication, the publisher will assign it to one of several freelance translators they work with. The translator first translates the material as closely as possible to get the literal meaning correct. This draft is then edited by both the translator and the editor to smooth out areas that are difficult to understand or that read awkwardly.

Translation, literary translation in particular, is not simply making a copy. There are close translations and loose translations. There are as many translations as there are translators. All translators bring with them knowledge, experience, and viewpoints which make them unique, and thus the material they translate will be unique. The literary translator must not only convey the identical meaning expressed by the author, but render the work in a literary style that flows smoothly, is easy to read, and is interesting to readers. The translation is as important as the book itself. A poorly written translation can destroy the work's literary appeal and kill its sales. It is therefore important that the literary translator possess excellent writing skills.

For book translation the amount you are paid depends on the difficulty of the work and the financial position of the publisher. For a short book which might take four to six weeks to translate, you could be paid about $3000.

A major export of the United States that also requires literary translation is films. Scripts and books by foreign authors must be translated into English. Scripts are reworked to fit the spoken language and slang of the country they are intended for, enabling audiences to accept the translation comfortably. Translators are also commonly used in writing subtitles to foreign films imported into the United States, and American films exported for distribution abroad. Dubbing of English speaking films is almost never done in the United States.

American companies that do subtitling usually use native speakers of the language in which the film is subtitled. The amount paid to translators is about $85-$120 per reel, with the average film length being 10-12 reels.

The Translation Committee of PEN American Center offers a booklet titled *A Handbook for Literary Translators*. It includes important information for literary translators, including a sample contract between translator and publisher. If you're interested in literary translation, this booklet is a must. You can get a copy of it by writing PEN American Center, 568 Broadway, New York, NY 10012.

BUSINESS OF FREELANCE TRANSLATING

Translators are expected to deliver clear, double-spaced copy of the completed work to clients within a specified time frame. The goal is to produce an accurate, edited translation, adhering closely to the original text without additions or omissions, and ready for typesetting and publication without further revision.

Access to a computer is necessary because the nature of this business requires many editing changes in the process of translating.

Your initial success is only a matter of making your services known to potential clients. Contact businesses, government agencies, and other organizations that would most likely use your services. Send a cover letter, resume, and samples of your work, as discussed in Chapter 4. Advertise in trade journals and even your local newspaper. If you are serious about getting into this business, the phone book is the best advertising you can buy for your money. You may also consider direct mail to select businesses. Don't waste money mailing to just any business, only those most likely to need your services. For example, there are thousands of publishers in this country, but only a few hundred are actively involved in obtaining foreign works. Although many publishers may have an occasional need for translation services, it probably would not be economical to approach them all directly. The best approach to publishers is an ad in a trade journal rather than using bulk mail unless you can get a mailing list of publishers who actively use foreign language services.

Perhaps your area, like most metropolitan areas, has commercial translating companies. Do not be intimidated by competing with them. As an independent your overhead expenses will be much lower, and therefore you can offer comparable services for less, allowing you to compete with them. You may even work with them. At times these companies may get overloaded and can subcontract out work to you. You may also do the same with them. If you have clients who need services you cannot provide but the translating service can, or if you are too busy to handle the load, you can subcontract work to them.

Translating bureaus usually do not employ a large, full-time staff of translators, but prefer to work with freelancers and assign work as need demands. So these agencies can also be sources of income for you.

The rate of pay is usually based on every 1000 words translated. For freelancers it can vary from $20 to $100 per 1000 words. A rate of 3000-4000 words a day is typical. However, 1000 words a day may be the maximum for a difficult text.

You might also consider a "Professional Errors and Omission" policy, or some other appropriate form for protection tailored to the needs of a freelance translating service. Check this out with your insurance broker or lawyer.

TRAINING AND ADDITIONAL RESOURCES

You may be saying to yourself, "These opportunities are promising, but the last time I had any foreign language training was years ago in high school. I could never do this type of work." Not so! This opportunity is not just for those who majored in foreign language in school. Opportunities are available to everyone regardless of current educational background. With the proper training and skill, you can become a translator. Even if you took your classes some years ago, once you start relearning and reviewing the language, it will come back to you.

Community education programs, colleges, private teaches, and business schools offer language classes. It is best to work for a degree, but not necessary, especially if your goal is to become a freelance translator. Concentrate on the core classes in the foreign language of interest. Also, listen to foreign language television and radio broadcasts. If you are interested in Spanish, this is easily accomplished as most metropolitan areas in the United States have Spanish speaking broadcasts. Communicate as much as possible with people who speak the language.

For someone interested primarily in translating, one of the most important things to do is read! Read books and magazines in the language. Check the library for available materials and resources. Subscribe to foreign language periodicals and read them regularly. The best way to learn how to read and write a language is to read and write the language, so practice as much as possible. Join language organizations. Do volunteer work for civic, religious, educational, and professional groups to perfect your skills. Volunteer work will also provide you with business references in the future. This work is a good way to get your foot in the door, as many of these organizations have connections with businesses and organizations that hire freelance translators.

Your translating skills will be more valuable if you also possess skills in other areas such as engineering, finance, medicine, etc.

Plan out your educational goals. It may take only a year of refresher courses or require four intensive years of study, but regardless, it can open up an exciting new freelance career for you. According to a job service based in San Francisco, the leading languages that will be vital to United States businesses over the next two decades are, in order, Spanish, Japanese, French, Chinese, German, and Russian. There is also a high demand for Italian, Portuguese, and Polish. Eastern European languages will become more important as those countries move toward democracy, and their foreign interaction increases.

Spanish is the second language of the world. It is also the second dominant language in the United States. If you are looking for a language that has high potential, Spanish may be it. Spanish is easier to learn for English speaking people than most other languages, and opportunities to study and develop proficiency are everywhere. Spanish classes are offered in virtually every U.S. city; it is easy to find those who speak it; and literature is readily available. Demographic projections show the percentage of native Spanish speakers will increase dramatically over the next two decades in the U.S. With a rise in Spanish speaking people will also come an increase in the need for those who can communicate in both Spanish and English.

I highly recommend joining the American Translators Association. The aim of this organization is to promote the recognition of translating as a profession, to advocate and maintain standards of professional ethics, practices, and competence, and to improve the standards and quality of translating. The American Translators Association also offers a test to members for accreditation. Accreditation supplies proof of competence and professionalism to potential clients. The test is open book and consists of five passages, one in each of the following categories: general, literary, legal or business, scientific or medical, and semitechnical. Candidates are expected to complete three passages of their choice within three hours. Practice tests are also available, which are graded in the same manner as the accreditation tests.

Other organizations of interest include the American Literary Translators Association and American Association of Language Specialists (see the appendix for addresses). I also recommend reading some of the many books discussing career opportunities available to translators.

An informative booklet titled *Translator Training Guidelines*, and a list of schools offering training for translators, are available from the American Translators Association.

CHAPTER 11

INDEXING

A person who creates an index is called an indexer. The majority of indexers are hired by publishing companies and work at home as freelancers. Indexing is one of those services most people do not even know exists. It is considered unusual because it is not a service most ordinary people use or can appreciate. However, those businesses that use indexers recognize the value of the service. Indexing provides a wonderful opportunity for freelancers. Most nonfiction books contain an index to help readers find specific material in the text. Nonfiction books include how-to, self-help, cookbooks, and school and college textbooks, all of which should contain an index. Many magazines index all of their articles annually. Nonfiction books comprise the largest category of books published. Having an index is very important and often it is the deciding factor by a customer whether a book is purchased or not, especially by librarians and teachers. So, indexing is an important aspect of book production. Can you imagine trying to find a reference to Myles Standish in a history book without an index!

THE INDEXING PROCESS

In order to compile the index, the indexer must read through the text, making a list of names, key words, and phrases and noting the page numbers where they occur. The words and phrases the indexer lists can be entered in a computer or put on 3 x 5-inch cards and stacked in alphabetical order. The completed list will be either typed or placed on a computer printout, depending on which of the above methods are used.

The client gives the indexer what is called a "galley" of the book. The galley is a prepublication copy of the text laid out in book format exactly as it will be published. This way the page numbers are fixed and each word, phrase, or reference can be identified with a page number that will be the same when the book is published. Indexing is done after most of the editing has been completed but can also be done before or after final proofreading. Some indexers proofread as well, and combine their duties, eliminating the need for another person to do the job and thus cutting costs and reducing time necessary to prepare the book for publication.

The indexer must select all pertinent words from the text to create a useful index. Most front and back matter of the book such as the title page, dedication, list of tables and illustrations, acknowledgments, glossary, bibliography, etc. should not be indexed. The only exceptions would be appendixes, prefaces, and forewords which should only be indexed if they contain important material omitted from the body of the text.

Materials needed by the indexer include several hundred 3 x 5-inch index cards, alphabetic tab dividers for the cards, a file box to hold the cards, and a typewriter or computer. On each card the indexer will write a key word, name, or phrase and the page number. The card is then filed in alphabetical order in the file box. You may use as few as two or three cards per page of text or as many as 10 cards per page depending of the complexity of the text. On average, you can expect to use between 500 to 1000 cards for each book.

Once all entries have been made on the cards you need to make cross-references, group subentries, and final decisions on the use of terms. The cards are then retyped on 8½ x 11-inch paper and double spaced. Entries should form one column on the page with extra spaces separating the sections of the alphabet, so that the A entries are separated from the B entries, and the B entries from the C entries and so on. If you have a computer with an indexing program this entire process is greatly simplified. Deliver one copy of your index to your client and keep a copy for your records. The second copy is kept in case the first is lost or if the client calls with a question.

Indexers can be paid by the page, hour, or project. Some indexers with special training or schooling will specialize in a certain field, such a medicine or engineering. This special training will merit a higher rate of pay.

TYPES OF INDEXES

If you look at the indexes in several different books you will notice that they vary slightly in style and format. The differences arise because of the subject matter of the text, author's style, or publisher's preferences. Some indexes simply list key words and page numbers while others are very detailed and may even include a description or definition of the words and extensive cross-references.

The type of indexes you create and the format you use will depend on the project and what the client wants.

Scholarly works often contain more than one index. One index would be of a general nature while the others would focus on particular aspects of the subject material. A history book, for example, which contains numerous references to historical figures may include a separate index of just names. A text which contains information on many authors and their works may have a separate index listing only the authors and another listing their works. Books of poetry or music may include and index of titles, first lines, or authors, or some combination of these.

The primary purpose of all these types of indexes is to provide a useful and easy to use reference for the reader. All indexes should be created with this goal in mind.

MECHANICS OF INDEXING

At first glance creating an index does not look difficult, and it isn't, but there is more to it than you might think. Indexing is not just placing a bunch of words in alphabetical order. There is a system that must be followed in order to make the index meaningful and useful for the reader.

In this section I will explain the basic rules or mechanics for creating a index. With this knowledge you will know how to properly prepare a generalized index. References for additional index training and knowledge are provided at the end of the chapter.

An entry is the principal word or phrase listed in an index. It is accompanied by a page reference where the subject is discussed in the text. Entries are listed in alphabetical order. The first word in the entry is usually capitalized. An exception to this is in scientific texts where lower case is used. The following is a sample index listing.

Encyclopedia, 19-22
Essays, 10, 11, 12
Experts, 342
Fairy tales, 223-26
Film reviews, 34
Foreign literary works, 59
Government documents, 210, 215

When the subject entry is continually discussed for more than one page, the beginning and ending reference pages are given (i.e., Encyclopedia, 19-22). If, however, individual references to the subject are made on a series of pages, each page is listed (i.e., Essays, 10, 11, 12).

Also note that when an entry includes a continuous series of pages, if the beginning page is 100 or greater, the ending page number is abbreviated. In the "Fairy tales" entry, the subject covers pages 223 through 226 but the page listing is given as 223-26. Entries which are closely related to each other are frequently grouped together under a main entry. All entries which have a long list of page references should be divided into subentries. This is done to help the reader. Entries with a long list of page references force the reader to search through many pages before finding the needed information. If, for example, you wanted to locate information about college libraries in the listing below you would have to check each reference.

Libraries, 6, 12-19, 23-27, 32-33, 38, 102, 108-11, 187-88

Having the references listed in subentries, as shown on the following page, makes finding the appropriate page references much easier. Any entry which has five or more page references should be divided into subentries.

Libraries
    academic, 23-27
    as picture sources, 187-88
    college, 102, 108-11
    depository, 99
    history of, 6
    museum, 32-33, 38
    public, 12-19

All indexes are set in what is referred to as a *flush-and-hang* format. The first line is set flush to the left margin and subsequent lines of that entry are indented below it. There are two different styles which are used with subentries. These are called *run-in* and *indented*. Run-in entries follow one another without breaks. See the example below.

Canada: agriculture and livestock, 55-59;
economy, 66; geography 60; industrial
development in the 19th century, 81-83;
political history, 82-88

Indented style lists each subentry on a separate line. Each line of the subentry is indented. See the following example.

Canada
  agriculture and livestock, 55-59
  economy, 66
  geography 60
  industrial development in the
    19th century, 81-83
  political history, 82-88

When two or more words can describe an entry, a cross-reference is used. The main entry will be the term most frequently used in the text. Other terms will be listed with a cross-reference to the main entry. If, for example, Soviet Union is used in the text, the full name Union of Soviet Socialist Republics will be listed but direct the reader to the main heading as shown.

Union of Soviet Socialist Republics, *see* Soviet Union

When a topic has closely related subjects in the same text, this information may also be included.

Horoscopes, 23-35; *see also* Astrology; Zodiac

Cross-references are indicated by the words *see* and *see also* and are set in italics for easy identification.
Personal names are listed by the surnames.

Jameson, William T., 145-49
Jones, Josiah, 304

Personal names should be listed as they are used in the text and as they are familiarly known. See the following examples.

Wells, H.G. (*not* Wells, Herbert George)
Stevenson, Robert Louis (*not* Stevenson, Robert L.)

If a person can be listed under two names, use the one most frequently used in the text and cross-reference the other. Jonathan Chapman, for example, is more popularly known as Johnny Appleseed. Page references would be listed under Johnny Appleseed, and Chapman would be cross-referenced as follows:

Chapman, Jonathan, *see* Johnny Appleseed

To aid the reader, explanatory notes are sometimes added in parentheses for select words:

Mexican War (1846-48), 67-80
Peppy (singing dog), 55
Yugasie (Indian brave), 456

Explanatory notes may be necessary when an entry can be confused with another one. For example, when the same names can indicate more than one person, place, or thing.

Smith, James (author), 52
Smith, James (physicist), 200

Mississippi (state), 33
Mississippi (river), 63

Acronyms and abbreviations of organizations should be indexed according to the abbreviations commonly used.

NATO, 50
NCAA, 94
YMCA, 190

In some cases the full name can accompany the abbreviation.

AMA (American Medical Association), 342

Often, there is more than one acceptable form of spelling for a word, for example, archaeology and archeology. Also some words have a British and an American spelling (i.e., colour and color). The spelling used in the index should be consistent with that used in the text.

Proper names are an important element of an index, but not every name mentioned in the text should be listed in the index. Doing so would clutter it with useless entries and make it less effective. An example from a book might read: "In an effort to find a climate where his tuberculosis might be controlled Robert Louis Stevenson traveled to Tahiti, Hawaii, and Samoa." Tahiti, Hawaii, and Samoa are mentioned here in the text but would be useless if included in an index. Casual or passing mention of people, places, and creative works (books, songs, plays, etc.) should not be included in the index.

A good indexer will try to anticipate the needs of the reader and will include and arrange information that will be most helpful.

ADDITIONAL RESOURCES AND TRAINING

Indexing is not difficult to learn. An indexer does not need to be an editor or possess the same degree of skill an editor or proofreader does in English usage and mechanics. You don't need a college degree or have any formal training to be an indexer. All you really need is a love for reading and an eye for detail. You can learn a great deal about indexing just by examining the indexes in various published books. In this chapter you have learned all the basic principles of indexing. For a more detailed study of the mechanics of indexing I would recommend that you see the chapter on indexing in *The Chicago Manual of Style*.

You may also take classes on the subject at colleges offering degrees in library science. If your local college does not have a library science program you can take a correspondence course from a college that does. To find out about local and correspondence college courses in library science talk to your local librarian. The library should have the reference material available to help you out.

You can give yourself more credibility to potential clients as an indexer if you are a member of the American Society of Indexers.

The American Society of Indexers was founded in 1968. It has approximately 800 members and eight regional groups. Members include professional indexers, librarians, editors, publishers, and organizations employing indexers. The purpose of the association is to improve the quality of indexing and indexing standards, to encourage members to increase their professional indexing capabilities and performance, to provide a means of communication, and to learn about new methods and developments in the field. The association sponsors workshops and seminars.

People interested in this profession should join this organization and attend the society's meetings and annual conferences to increase knowledge in the field and have the opportunity of networking with others in the profession.

Other organizations of interest to indexers are the Indexing and Abstracting Society of Canada, American Society for Information Science, and National Federation of Abstracting and Information Services. See the appendix for addresses to these organizations.

In the past most indexing jobs have been with book publishers, but opportunities are available now with magazine publishers and companies that produce catalogs. With the growth of the small press and desktop publishing industry, the market for potential freelance indexers has never been better and will continue to grow.

CHAPTER 12

LITERARY REPRESENTATION

Every year hundreds of thousands of writers seek publication of their works. Most of these are novice writers who have little knowledge of how, what, where, or who to submit their material. They do not know how to properly prepare their submissions. They do not know what type of book can and cannot be marketed profitably. And many of them do not know how to write, at least well enough for commercial purposes. Consequently, most of them will never become published.

Because publishers are flooded with unsuitable or unacceptable manuscripts, many refuse to even look at unsolicited material. The only way to reach these publishers is through a literary agent. The agent's job is to sift through all of these manuscripts and extract only those with promise. Agents relieve publishers of the task of reading and searching through mounds of manuscripts for those few worthy of consideration.

Agents consequently spend most of their time reading manuscripts. If they feel a writer has written a marketable manuscript, they will represent the author and the work by actively seeking a publisher to publish it. Most writers lack the knowledge necessary to find a suitable publisher. Many simply do not want to spend the time seeking out a publisher or negotiating a contract. Agents know what can sell and who to sell it to. Agents also know the publishing industry and can approach the best markets and negotiate the best terms for the author. Agents usually specialize in certain types of books, such as cookbooks, science fiction, screenplays, finance, and the like. Many will handle more than just one genre of book. Few handle a wide variety and those agencies that do, have agents who specialize. This allows the agent to be more effective. They learn which publishers are involved in their particular area of specialization, what the publishers' needs are, and they make personal contacts with the in-house editors. This close, personal contact helps keep agents in tune with publishers' needs and wants.

THE LITERARY AGENT BUSINESS

It goes without saying that literary agents spend a great deal of their time reading. They are continually searching for salable manuscripts and may read dozens of manuscripts before finding one they would be willing to represent.

When an agent finds a manuscript he feels has publishing potential, he will accept it for representation. The author is sent a contract or letter of agreement specifying the agent's commission, fees, and terms of the agreement. When that is signed, the agent begins seeking out suitable publishers to purchase the rights to the manuscript.

The agent does not send material out to just any publisher, but chooses the most appropriate for the manuscript. Not all publishers publish all types of books. Most publishers focus on certain types of books. For example, Players Press is interested only in books on or about performing arts and related topics. Writer's Digest Books publishes books on writing. All publishers have specific interests. It does no good to send a potential best selling cookbook to a music publisher. Agents know what publishers want. This information is given in directories like *Writer's Market* and *Novel and Short Story Writer's Market* and agents become very familiar with them. The agent sends out query letters and book proposals to chosen publishers. When a publisher shows interest, terms are negotiated and a contract is signed by all concerned parties. The publisher draws up the contract to be approved and signed by the author and agent.

Literary agents are paid a 10 to 20 percent commission on sales they make, 15 percent being the most common for sales within the country, and 20 percent for sales outside the country. The commission is paid on all royalties earned by the author. Usually, the publisher will send the royalty check to the agent, who then deducts his commission and forwards the rest to the author. If, for instance, an agent charges a 15 percent commission and the author receives a total of $10,000, his earnings would be $1,500. If the book happens to be a very good seller and earns $100,000, the agent gets $15,000—not a bad profit on a single book. You can imagine the potential with a million copy best seller!

It is therefore in the agent's best interest to get as large a royalty as possible, but royalties are not the only consideration; advances are equally important. Advances are part of the royalty paid to the author before the book is available for sale. They are usually paid after the contract is signed and the completed manuscript is delivered to the publisher. It is to the advantage of the author and agent to get as large an advance as possible. The reason is that many books fail to earn more than the advance amount. The advance is usually nonrefundable (if the book is published), so if the book does not sell enough to equal the advance, the agent and author come out ahead. This is a real concern because 80 percent of all new books published each year fail to make the publisher a profit and go out of print.

Most agents concentrate on book-length manuscripts only. The money for short stories, poetry, and magazine articles is usually too small for them to bother with. A few do handle articles and other short pieces, but only for well known authors seeking publication in the largest and highest paying magazines.

Agents aren't expected to be magicians. They cannot sell an unsalable manuscript. They also do not normally edit manuscripts, although they may offer this service separately. Usually, they leave the editing up to the author and publisher, although they do offer suggestions and advice on improving manuscripts. All manuscripts should be read by freelance editors and proofreaders before they are submitted to publishers. Agents can perform this service themselves or refer clients to freelancers to do the job. Editing will not only improve the manuscript, but greatly improve the chances of having the work accepted for publication.

Established literary agents, like publishers, are flooded with unsolicited manuscripts. For this reason they spend most of their time reading rather than marketing books. Although they may be representing 20 or 30 different clients at a time, not all of the manuscripts they work with get published. Because of this, many agents supplement their commission income by charging the authors fees. Some agents require fees from unpublished writers only. Some agents charge a marketing or consulting fee to all clients to cover the cost of postage and telephone expenses. Since most new writers are not lucky enough to get published, the chances that an agent will sell a novice writer's material are not good. Many of the old, well established literary agencies and agents will not consider representing unpublished authors. Most of the agents who are willing to work with unpublished authors usually charge them a fee for doing so as compensation for their time and effort.

Many agents offer consultation services, which are available to anybody. This service is to advise authors on book contracts for manuscripts they have sold without the help of an agent. These fees range from $20-$200 per hour.

Many agents will also charge a reading fee. The fee can vary anywhere from $40 to $300 or more. This is a fee the author pays just to have the agent read the manuscript. It is paid to the agent to compensate him for his time spent in reading, and not for representation. The agent is not expected to evaluate the manuscript or make any suggestions on improvement. It is just a payment for reading the manuscript. If the agent feels the manuscript can be sold, he will offer to represent the author and attempt to sell it to a publisher. Whether he accepts the manuscript or not, the agent still is paid the reading fee. Often agents will refund the reading fees if they are able to make a sale. Some agents will accept almost any manuscript offered to them and charge a large reading fee, also called a representation or consulting fee. Some of the less successful agents make most of their money this way.

Another fee commonly charged by literary agents is a criticism fee, which can range up to $400 or more. It involves not only reading the manuscript, but writing a detailed evaluation or critique for the author. In this sense the agent also functions as a literary critic. He combines the functions of two types of readers, agent and critic, to enhance his services.

Most of the older or more established literary agencies do not charge their clients reading fees. However, they are also much more selective and will not represent any writer unless he or she has already had several books published. Therefore, most new authors are restricted to agents who are willing to take a risk, but who will also probably charge a reading fee.

Almost all agents charge a marketing fee, as it is frequently called. This fee covers expenses in marketing the author's material. It will include postage, phone and fax, photocopying, express mail expenses, and the like. Usually a set amount, such as $20 or $40, is charged for each book the agent represents.

BECOMING A LITERARY AGENT

Literary agents are basically brokers. They bring buyers (publishers and production companies) and sellers (writers) together. No experience, college degree, special testing, or training is required to become a literary agent. But that doesn't mean anybody can just call themselves an agent and go out looking for clients. You still need to possess a certain amount of skill and knowledge before you can start. Most agents have gained their initial experience and background working as editors, book buyers, publishers' sales reps, publicists, or as published authors themselves. Some start on the ground floor, working in a literary agency. If you have experience in any of these fields, you should have some valuable background knowledge to start with. If not, you can learn the trade just as many other agents have—as an author. Learn the submission process. Even though many large publishers will not work with unagented authors, many still do, and any author can, and most still do, prepare and submit their own work. Learning how to do this is not difficult. You can learn the process by reading a few chapters in any book on getting published (I even give you the basic information you need in this book).

However, to be a successful agent you must have a sense of what can and cannot sell and who to sell it to. You must know what type of books are marketable and can make money for a publisher. After all, publishers are in business to make money, not create literary masterpieces or feed starving authors. They will publish only those books they believe will make them the most profit. Good book ideas and plots are not enough. Good topics and plots are worthless if the writer does not have adequate literary skill. The reverse is also true—good writing in itself is not enough. You must have a capable author with a marketable idea. Often an agent can give the author constructive criticism, and with the aid of a copy editor, mold the writer's work into something that is salable.

When you first start out as an agent, you will need to build up a clientele of authors. Successful agents rely almost totally on referrals from satisfied clients and personal contacts for the majority of their authors. Established agents also get queries constantly through the mail, as a result of being listed in trade and association directories. Most new agents must rely on advertising until they become established. The most important place to advertise is the phone book, as many writers will look there first. You can also place inexpensive advertisements in writers' magazines. Since authors are always looking for agents to represent them, advertising will bring a slew of inquiries. The really successful agents avoid advertising simply because they are already deluged with submissions from writers and can pick and choose who their clients.

If you want to become a literary agent, you must first become very familiar with the process of submitting book proposals and working with publishers. I recommend that as you start out in this business, since you will probably be inexperienced, you adjust your fees accordingly and readjust them as your skills improve. Many budding authors will be happy to work with you if you charge only for expenses such as postage and stationery and avoid upfront fees. Of course, a commission would also be expected.

I also recommend you try getting some of your own writing published and experience firsthand what is involved in the process before attempting to sell someone else's work. Experience is a wonderful teacher. You need to be professional in your approach to publishers or you will look just as bad as a novice writer who isn't sure what he is doing. A good agent can provide a wonderful service to writers. However, a bad agent is worse than no agent at all, and I have seen many bad agents. Bad in the sense that they don't know what they are doing or don't follow standard practices, acting more like pesky salespeople than courteous professionals. Don't give publishers hard sell tactics or claim your client's book is a potential best seller—no one can predict that. The experts are often proved wrong. Present the material and let the publisher decide whether it is right for them or not.

BOOK PROPOSALS

Besides providing the author with constructive criticism, seeking out publishers, and negotiating publishing agreements for clients, another function of literary agents is to help clients properly prepare their material for submission to publishers. Most writers, particularly novices, who make up the vast majority of those seeking publication, do not know how to properly prepare a book proposal, format a manuscript, or effectively approach a publisher, despite the fact that most books on the topic of getting published—and there are many of them—contain this information. As an agent you could help a new writer tremendously just by providing this basic knowledge.

A book proposal is usually the first thing you will send to a book publisher to interest him in your manuscript. Do not send the complete manuscript unless it is requested. A book proposal is some combination of a cover letter (or query letter), a synopsis, an outline, and sample chapters. The exact combination of these will depend on the publisher, as indicated in *Writer's Market*. Some publishers use the terms "synopsis" and "outline" interchangeably. Most publishers will request either a synopsis or an outline, but not usually both.

The author will prepare all the materials except the cover or query letter, which should be written by the agent. Most book publishers will accept book proposals as their initial contact, or request a proposal in response to a query letter. You will need to learn how to write effective query letters and prepare good book proposals.

Cover Letter

The cover letter in a book proposal is the same as a query letter (as described in Chapter 6) and contains basically the same information. It is a business letter written to the publisher by the agent. It is important you use your company letterhead, and state that you are representing the author so that the publisher will know you are an agent and give your material due respect.

Some publishers will desire only a query letter before being sent either a book proposal or the manuscript. The query letter acts as an introduction to you and your author's book idea. By sending a query letter first, you can find out if the publisher has any interest in the book. If an editor responds to a query with a request to see your material, he will be more receptive since he requested it.

Query letters and book proposals will keep your client's manuscript out of the slush pile. Many publishers put all unsolicited manuscripts aside into what is known as the slush pile. There they sit until they are returned to the author or until an editor who has some spare time rummages through the stack. In either case, having a submission in the slush pile is not to the writer's benefit. When you send a book proposal or manuscript, always include a cover letter. If you are sending the material on the publisher's request, the cover letter should not be a repeat of your query letter or used to make a sales pitch. Keep it to only a paragraph or two and just briefly remind the editor that he requested the material.

Synopsis
A synopsis is a very brief summary of your book. If it is a novel, it should cover the basic plot or theme and reveal the ending. Make the synopsis interesting and easy to read. Limit it to two or three double-spaced pages.

Outline
The outline covers the highlights of your book chapter by chapter. Each chapter should begin on a separate page. If your outline is for a novel, include all major characters, the main plot, subplots, and any pertinent details. The outline should be several double-spaced pages in length and may be as long as 20 or more pages. You should have at least one full page written on each chapter.

Detailed outlines are especially important for manuscripts which are not yet complete. A thorough outline shows the editor you have thought about and researched the subject adequately, and can complete the manuscript. The problem editors want to avoid is accepting a manuscript idea that has only a few completed chapters with an outline of several additional chapters and discover that the author couldn't find much more to say in the final chapters, and end up with a skimpy 84 page book, or having the second half of the book turn into a philosophical platform inappropriate to the rest of the book, or some other such problem not anticipated by the editor. Having a detailed outline helps eliminate these problems. If it is a novel, the editor also wants to see if you can fully develop the story and maintain the reader's interest.

Although you will not include dialog or be too descriptive or flowery in the outline, you should make the material as interesting as possible. Editors don't want to read something dry and boring. Avoid using the passive voice. Focus on the action, characters, and plot.

Often, particularly with medium and large sized publishing houses, an in-house editor must convince superiors to buy the book. A well written outline will help him. The senior editors, who will probably never read the book, will make the decisions based on the junior editor's enthusiasm, marketing considerations, and the outline or synopsis.

Sample Chapters

Most publishers prefer to see sample chapters before requesting the entire manuscript. You should send three chapters unless specified otherwise in *Writer's Market*. Some publishers will indicate they want certain chapters, while others will leave that decision up to the author or agent. The publisher may require the first three chapters so they can see how the author develops the book. Others may want the first, a middle, and the last chapter to see how it begins, develops, and ends. Most publishers let you choose the chapters to send. The material should total between 40 to 60 pages. You need to send a sample large enough to show the author's skill.

Manuscript Submissions

If, after sending out a proposal or query letter, you get a positive response requesting a copy of the author's manuscript, you should include a cover letter. You have already sent your query letter and don't need to restate any of that information. Don't make a sales pitch. In the cover letter simply remind the editor that you are sending the manuscript on his request.

If you are submitting your manuscript to a publisher who considers complete manuscripts with the initial contact, your cover letter should give the editor a brief description of the book and tell him something about the author, his qualifications, and his publishing history—just like the query letter. You usually do not need to include a synopsis or an outline, but could if you think it would be helpful.

The manuscript should be prepared just as described in Chapter 6. Whether it's a book or an article, the manuscript should be formatted the same way. The only difference is a book-length manuscript would include a title page and begin each chapter one-third of a page from the top. It is important the manuscript be clean and neat. Don't send old, dog-eared manuscripts. A publisher who receives a worn manuscript automatically assumes it has been sent to, and rejected, by every other publisher in the business and is instantly biased against it. Make the manuscript look like new so the publisher believes he is the first to see it.

PUBLISHING AGREEMENTS

Many new writers are so happy to have a publisher accept their work that they would not dare take the risk of offending the publisher and jeopardize their chances of getting published by haggling over the terms of the contract. An experienced agent knows what can be negotiated and how far to push, usually upping the publisher's original offer to cover his commission and sometimes even more.

The thought of negotiating a publishing agreement, let alone understanding it, can be frightening to some people. Contracts in general are notoriously confusing, being overloaded with legal talk unfamiliar with most of us. Luckily, you don't need to be a lawyer to understand a book contract. Although, if you've never seen one before, you may be slightly confused.

Publishing agreements aren't difficult to understand if you have someone explain them to you. I won't spend much time on contracts because there is more to them than I can adequately include in this chapter. What I will do is refer you to an excellent book on the subject that is written in layman's language. The book is *How to Understand and Negotiate a Book Contract or Magazine Agreement* by Richard Balkin. The book pulls apart some publishing agreements and explains them section by section. It also explains the negotiating process and how to deal with a publisher to get the best possible terms. After reading this book you will have a good, basic understanding of publishing agreements and be able to intelligently read one. I consider this book a must for anyone interested in becoming a literary agent. The appendix lists other good books on this subject.

Remember, an agent is not expected to be a lawyer, but he is expected to understand publishing agreements. You can get a good grip on them by reading books on this topic and by reading agreements.

SCRIPT AGENTS

Perhaps you would like to take part in the creation of a major motion picture, popular TV series, or even a Broadway play. You can as a script agent. Script agents are a special type of literary agent who specialize in selling scripts to production companies and publishers.

Script agents typically get a 10 percent commission for domestic sales and 15 percent for foreign sales. Many literary agents are also script agents. The Writers Guild of America (WGA) prohibits signatory agencies from charging reading fees, but there is no restriction on offering supplementary services such as editing and critiquing. Most script agents are signatory members of the WGA because it gives them respectability and credibility

All script writers can benefit by using an agent because it is very difficult to sell a script without representation. Like book publishers, production companies are inundated with submissions and do not have the time to wade through piles of scripts sent to them. The agent selects only those scripts with potential. Some movie producers, theatrical companies, and publishers will accept unagented scripts, but television producers will not. Production companies are plagued with "nuisance" lawsuits, in which writers claim their scripts were stolen. To protect themselves, producers rely on agents to screen out nonprofessionals— the ones causing the problems.

If you are interested in becoming a script agent, you should consider subscribing to some of the newsletters and trade publications in order to keep in touch with what is happening in the industry. *Daily Variety* and *The Hollywood Reporter* are daily business papers of the entertainment industry. *The Hollywood Scriptwriter* is a newsletter aimed at new and professional scriptwriters. It includes agency updates along with an Annual Agency Issue every summer.

As a script agent you must be familiar with writing scripts as well as selling them. There are several good resources listed in the appendix about scriptwriting which you should become familiar with. The book *How to Sell Your Screenplay* by Carl Sautter, provides an excellent overview of preparing, submitting, and selling scripts. Other books of interest to script agents include *Making a Good Script Great* by Linda Seger, *Successful Scriptwriting* by Kerry Cox and Jurgen Wolff, and *Writing Screen Plays That Sell* by Michael Hauge (see the appendix).

ADDITIONAL RESOURCES

Literary agents learn their trade by experience. As I have explained, they are not required to have any special training or accreditation; however, membership in one of the trade organizations requires them to adhere to a code of ethics and standards, giving them some degree of recognition as professionals. The major organization for agents is the Association of Authors' Representatives, which by the way, prohibits most of its members from charging reading fees. A second organization, Writer's Guild of America, also has many agents as members. Agents and TV, radio, and motion picture producers can become members of the WGA by signing the guild's agreement on basic standards for the treatment of writers. Membership in one of these organizations will help improve your understanding of the profession and bring you more business. Many writers look at membership as a criteria in their search for an agent. Membership directories are available to anyone who sends a self-addressed stamped envelope. The addresses for these organizations can be found in the appendix.

You can also get listed in the following directories of agents: *Literary Agents of North America, Guide to Literary Agents and Art/Photo Reps, Literary Market Place,* and *Writers' & Artists' Yearbook.* These books can be located in the reference section of your local library. Write to the publishers and see what the requirements are to be listed. Most writers will go to these directories in search of an agent.

For additional information about literary agents I recommend reading *Literary Agents: A Writer's Guide,* by Debby Mayer, and *Literary Agents: How to Get and Work with the Right One for You,* by Michael Larsen. Although written from an author's perspective, they provide interesting and valuable information about literary agents and how they work.

CHAPTER 13

MANUSCRIPT READING

A few years ago the editors at Writer's Digest Books sent a survey to publishers asking them who reads their unsolicited manuscripts. The responses they received varied greatly and included "editor," "editorial assistant," "acquisitions editor," "publisher," and "editorial committee," among others. Also mentioned were "freelance readers." A significant number of companies that responded to the survey indicated that unsolicited manuscripts were read or screened by these freelance manuscript readers, rather than in-house editors.

Publishers and agents receive multitudes of unsolicited manuscripts daily. Because these people are so busy, the manuscripts are put aside until the editors have a few spare moments to spend time digging through the stack.

Some book publishers employ manuscript readers, also known as *first readers, editorial assistants,* or *editorial associates,* whose purpose is to read through all unsolicited material in search of something that has marketing potential. These people search through stacks and stacks of submissions. If they find something of interest, they will present it to their supervisor who, if interested, will present it to someone else higher up the ladder or to an editorial committee. Eventually, if the material is accepted, it will go on to publication.

In most small or medium sized publishing houses, the first reader is a staff member, either one of the editors or sometimes even the publisher. At large publishing companies, the first reader is typically someone in an entry-level editorial position. Many editors begin their careers as first readers.

Some publishing companies and literary agencies hire freelance readers to read their manuscripts. The freelance first reader or manuscript reader will read a manuscript and then write a one or two-page evaluation or book report, which will include a synopsis of the manuscript and the reader's recommendations. Most of the manuscripts publishers receive are poorly written and unmarketable, consequently they are rejected without a thorough reading. However, manuscripts that appear to have some promise are evaluated further, often by freelance manuscript readers. The first reader evaluates the book's potential in terms of writing quality and marketability. The primary concern of publishers is: Will the book make money? If it has the potential to be a good seller they will look at it further. If not, it will be passed up for another book that shows more promise.

Book clubs, television and motion picture studios, and talent agents also hire manuscript readers to screen both books and manuscripts. Book clubs and film producers, like publishers and literary agents, have potentially promising unsolicited and solicited manuscripts which must be evaluated. They also evaluate published books. Readers are assigned either manuscripts or books to evaluate. In the film industry, manuscript readers are commonly referred to as *story analysts*, and their evaluations are called *coverages*. Film makers and talent agents hire both full-time and freelance story analysts.

Reading manuscripts can be a fun and interesting experience. Since writers manifest a wide variety of talent and ideas, as a manuscript reader you will evaluate materials which span the spectrum from very good to very bad. Most of the material you read will never make it into print or onto film. The vast majority of manuscripts publishers and film producers receive are rejected. Only a small fraction of the material submitted to publishers is actually good enough to be published. The same is true with screenplays which eventually are made into films. The in-house first reader and the freelance manuscript reader are the ones who weed out most of the unpublishable manuscripts. Finding those few manuscripts that are producible is exciting.

Although no formal education is required to be a freelance manuscript reader, a college degree or prior editing or publishing experience is highly recommended. In fact, if you don't have a college degree or work experience within the publishing industry or other appropriate field, it is extremely difficult to land a job as a manuscript reader. Competition for available jobs is fierce, employers are very selective, and unqualified people have little chance to break into this field.

Manuscript readers must possess a basic understanding of the client's needs, and understand what works are marketable and potentially profitable. Prior experience as an editor can provide some of this background knowledge. A love for reading is not enough. Most people, including the average writer, do not really understand what can or can't be published or produced and marketed successfully. Having some experience in the book or film industry provides the background necessary to make educated evaluations on the potential of unpublished manuscripts. Besides editing experience, if you happen to be a published author, that indicates you have some degree of knowledge about the marketability of books or screenplays and how to write them. So a published author would also have the credentials to become a freelance manuscript reader.

Readers also need to be well read so they can compare the manuscripts they read to books and films of the same genre. If you've never read a western, for example, then how are you going to compare a manuscript of this type to books currently being published? This is true of any genre of book. If you do read a variety of topics, your chances of working as a reader are improved. For general reading, a college degree in English or literature would be beneficial. A degree would show the publisher you understand the language and know the difference between good and bad writing. Most publishers look for readers with special training or skills to read books in these areas. For example, a person with a college degree in business would read books on finance, or a teacher would read classroom textbooks. In fact, the best opportunities for manuscript readers in the publishing industry exist in special areas. If you have special training or experience, you have marketable skills that will help you get jobs as a manuscript reader. Textbook publishers probably use freelance manuscript readers more than any other type of publisher. If you are a teacher or have teaching experience in grade school, high school, or college, these publishers could use you to evaluate textbook manuscripts.

WRITING THE EVALUATION

If you are accepted as a manuscript reader, the publisher will send you appropriate manuscripts from time to time to read and evaluate. You will be expected to write a one to two-page evaluation of the manuscript, much like a book report. Although writing talent is not a requirement, you need to be able to express yourself clearly in writing. Your services are used to save the editor time, and if he cannot get a good judgement of the manuscript from your evaluation, your services will not be used again. Sometimes editors will assign new readers a manuscript "on spec," which means he is not obligated to pay you if your evaluation does not meet his standards. Frequently, new readers lack the ability to write clear, concise reports that are useful to the editor. This way the editor can test your ability. If your report is acceptable, you will get paid and receive additional assignments. If not, you will not get further assignments. You may volunteer to do your first project for free just to get your foot in the door and to show the client your skill.

Often clients will give readers a questionnaire or evaluation form to fill out which asks specific questions about the manuscript. This form provides questions the client needs to have answered about the manuscript in order to decide whether to reject it or pass it along for further evaluation. This is most common with textbook manuscripts. A sampling of the types of questions that could be asked regarding a manuscript for a school text are:

• Are all important topics covered?
• Is the book suitable for the grade level intended? If not, explain why.
• What are its strengths and weaknesses?
• Would the text organization fit the way the course is taught?
• Would this approach work with your students? Would you suggest any changes?
• Are the facts and methodology up-to-date?
• Are there features in the text that distinguish it from other texts?
• Would this book compete well with others already on the market? If not, why?
• What do you like most about the text?
• Is it written in a style that is clear and easy to read?
• Would you consider using this text for your class?
• What changes would you make, if any?

The reader simply answers these questions as completely as possible. When an evaluation form is not supplied by the publisher, you would simply write a book report.

Two other broad categories of books are fiction and nonfiction. Some of the questions you should answer for fictional (novel) and biographical book reports are:

• Explain the plot and subplots.
• Who are the major characters?
• What is the time period and the setting?
• Are the characters and plot developed well?
• Is the text easy to read and error free?

- What did you like most about the work?
- What did you like least about the work?
- How does it compare with other published books in the same genre?
- Does this book fit well with other books produced by this publisher? Why?
- If it is a biography, is any new information revealed?
- Who would buy this book?

Questions you would answer for a nonfiction (how-to, self-help) book report are:

- What is the scope and content of the book?
- Are instructions clear and easy to follow?
- Is the terminology and vocabulary suitable for its intended audience?
- Is the material presented in a readable and interesting manner?
- Is the material up-to-date and accurate? Is it well researched?
- What supporting information (photos, illustrations, graphs, tables, maps, appendixes, bibliographies, etc.) is used, and is it helpful?
- Who would buy this type of book? What markets would it appeal to?
- What makes this book different from others that may have been published on the same subject?
- Does the book adequately accomplish its purpose or objective?

Write your report answering questions like those above. Don't respond to these questions with just a simple one sentence answer; fully expound and explain your observations and impressions, yet keep your comments to the point. Do not use more words than is necessary. Clients usually do not want to trudge through a ten page essay. Your report needs to be detailed enough to give the editor a complete and accurate overview of the book.

You may not be given a questionnaire but simply be asked to write a synopsis of the book describing the events in the story as they happen. This might be accompanied by a list and description of the main characters. You would conclude with a few of your own comments about the story and the author's writing ability.

APPROACHING MARKETS

Send your potential clients a cover letter, a resume, and samples of your work. All correspondence and all book reviews must be typewritten or from a computer with a letter quality printer.

In the cover letter you will offer your services as a manuscript reader. Briefly describe any pertinent skills, schooling, or training you have that qualifies you for the job. Editors are very busy people so keep the letter to only a few paragraphs and no longer than a page.

Include a copy of your resume as described in Chapter 4. Also enclose one of your book evaluations as a sample of your work. If you have a completed review from a previous client, use a copy of it. If not, use one of your practice reviews. If you are just starting out as a reader, you wouldn't be expected to have anything other than your own practice reviews, so don't claim them as actual samples of reports you have done for clients. Since you may use samples of your book reports for future inquiries with employers, it is a good practice to keep copies of all of those you write.

Your chances of finding publishers who are willing to hire you are greatly improved if you study their companies and know exactly what types of materials they publish. You should also familiarize yourself with the publications of other publishers who publish similar books, to know the competition and quality of the materials in print. Since it is impossible to know about all types of books, you should specialize in a topic which interests you or in which you have training or experience. You can choose two or maybe even three related fields, but don't try to bite off more than you can chew. The number of books published in many of these categories each year is more than most people can keep up with. Even within publishing companies editors specialize in certain types of books so they can adequately judge the needs and trends of the marketplace within their area of specialization.

If you want to work as a manuscript reader for a publishing company, you might want to choose an area of specialization. Read as many of the books in this area that you can find. If you chose a topic you already have an interest in or are involved in professionally, you probably have already read many of these books. To find which books are available, go to your local library and see what they have on the shelves. The library, however, will only stock a few selected titles of any type of book. Although the titles they stock are usually recommended by book reviewers and are some of the best available, they will not have all the books that are available, nor will they necessarily have all of the best books. You can find out what books are currently in print by looking in a directory titled *Books in Print*, which is available in most libraries. This reference lists every book which publishers currently have in print and available for sale. You can look up books by topic. You may want to look up several related topics so you can find as many books of interest as possible. You can then make a list of all the books in print on your subject of interest. Read as many of these as you have the time and interest to do. You can acquire these books in the library, through interlibrary loan, at a bookstore, or even directly from the publisher.

The entries in *Books in Print* will give you the title of the book, the publisher's name, and other information. Make a list of all the publishers. This will serve as your list of potential clients. Look up each of the publishers in *Writer's Market*. This reference will briefly describe each company and the types of books they publish. Most publishers offer author guidelines which describe in greater detail the types of books they publish. You can get a copy of these guidelines and a copy of their catalog by sending a stamped self-addressed 9 x 12-inch envelope. Many publishers give exact postage requirements and envelope size in their listing in *Writer's Market*. If you do not know how much postage to put on the envelop, use enough for a 16 oz. package.

Study the materials for each of the publishers you are interested in working with. Then, send them a letter of inquiry to see if they hire freelance manuscript readers. State your areas of expertise and any schooling, training, or experience you have that shows your qualifications. The key to landing this type of reading job is to have the proper background and experience, knowing exactly what types of books the publisher is interested in, and having a knowledge of what is currently in print.

EMPLOYMENT OUTLOOK

Publishers, literary and talent agents, theater, television, and stage production companies, and book clubs use readers. However, finding jobs with these companies is not easy.

Unless you have special training or prior experience in the industry (publishing, theater, etc.), you will find it very difficult to find a job as a reader. More and more of the larger publishing houses and film production companies are relying on literary and script agents to screen their submissions and, in effect, do the job freelance readers do. Also, almost all publishers recommend or even require authors themselves to submit summaries or outlines of their books before sending in the complete manuscript, thereby diminishing the need to hire readers for this job. Although the job opportunities for manuscript readers are becoming difficult to find, publishers and film producers still hire qualified freelancers.

Many of the companies that once hired manuscript readers do not anymore because literary agents are performing this task for them. Some agents perform this service themselves, but many hire freelance readers to do it for them. As more and more publishers require authors to submit their material through agents, the need for manuscript readers will increase—not among publishers, but among agents.

The opportunities for manuscript readers are greater with literary agents than with publishing and production companies. Hiring manuscript readers creates just another expense for publishers, so most now rely on employees or agents. Agents, on the other hand, can afford to hire manuscript readers because the cost of this service is absorbed by the author. Reading fees are charged to the author by the agent. In fact, the agent could even make money in the process, if he charges more than what he pays the reader.

Not all agents charge their clients reading fees. Those who don't normally do not hire manuscript readers. Some directories which list agents such as the *Guide to Literary Agents and Art/ Photo Reps,* specify which agents charge reading fees. Your best chance of finding a job as a manuscript reader would be by contacting these agents. If you have a college degree, particularly an advanced degree or a degree in English, you have a fair chance of finding work as a manuscript reader.

An important factor involved in hiring freelance manuscript readers is location. Television and motion picture studios, talent agencies, and film production companies look primarily for readers who live in their vicinity. Sending manuscripts out of town is an unnecessary expense and a waste of time. Many clients want the evaluations or coverages within a couple of days. The mail alone would take a week round trip, unless sent by express, which is too expensive. Add onto that a couple of days for the reading and writing of the evaluation may be longer than most clients want to wait. To some extent this is also true with publishing companies and literary agents as well.

The most likely cities for finding a job as a manuscript reader would be New York and Los Angeles because both of these areas are primary centers of book publishing and film production in North America. Florida and Illinois (particularly Chicago) are are two other areas where these industries are growing. Readers should first look for jobs with publishing or film producers in their own community. However, some companies will work with freelancers entirely through the mail.

Probably the most responsive publishers for readers to approach are textbook publishers. They need qualified people to read and evaluate textbook manuscripts. If you are a teacher, your chances of finding work as a reader are better than most, but you must contact publishers directly rather than literary agents. Literary agents do not usually handle textbooks, partly because authors of these types of books are usually familiar enough with the textbook publishers to approach them themselves.

RESOURCES

I recommend that anyone interested in working as a manuscript reader should study books on writing book reports or book reviews. There should be many such books available in your local library. One particular book which may be of help to you is *How to Read a Book* by Mortimer Adler and Charles Van Doren. This is a classic text on how to analyze books. Other good resources are listed in the appendix.

If you are interested in becoming a story analysts for a talent agency or film production company, you should be familiar with how to write screenplays. There are many good books available on this subject, some of which are listed on page 174 and in the appendix. Another good resource is *Reading for a Living: How to Be a Professional Story Analyst for Film and Television* by T. L. Katahn. This book was written by a working story analyst and provides considerable detail about the job. It also includes several sample coverages or evaluations as examples.

If you live in Los Angeles or New York where the film industry is strong, you may be able to take a class in story analysis at a local college which has a film or theater department. The American Film Institute in Los Angeles offers such a class. Other schools and universities around the country may offer similar classes, as well as classes in screenwriting which would also be very beneficial.

CHAPTER 14

OTHER READING JOBS

I have included the following jobs for readers into a single chapter because the opportunities that exist for them are limited. Most of the reader jobs mentioned in this chapter will be part-time, and generally the jobs or clients will be harder to find. However, these opportunities do exist and some people have been able to make satisfying full and part-time careers doing them. For this reason, I have included them in this book. If any of them sound like something you would like to do, then by all means you should consider pursuing them.

STUDENT READER

This opportunity is only one of the few described in this book in which you can just sit back and make money purely by reading. Most all other types of readers require some type of additional work. All a student reader does is read and get paid for it. This is truly one of those money-making opportunities most anyone can cash in on without having any special training or qualifications and without doing additional work. It is also the best and most readily available reading opportunity listed in this chapter. A student reader's job is to read books to students, usually college students who have physical handicaps that limit their reading ability. Many colleges and universities offer this type of program to their handicapped students. Students who are visually impaired (although not necessarily blind) need people to read their school assignments to them, so colleges hire readers to help them with their education.

To be a student reader requires no special skills except the ability to read. No editing or proofreading knowledge or report writing is required, and no college degree is needed. If you can read the student's textbooks, you can qualify as a reader. This is an opportunity most anyone with a love for reading can do to earn extra income. All the reader does is contact the students and arrange for a time and place convenient to do the reading.

Go to the administration office of your local college, university, or high school and see if they offer a reading program for disabled students. Not all colleges have these types of programs. If you are hired to work in such a program, you can expect to be paid by the school and not by the individual student. You are employed by the school rather than the student, although some students may hire readers as well. You work as a part-time independent contractor for the school and therefore do not qualify for employee benefits, provided only to full-time employees.

CLIPPING SERVICE READERS

Readers are used all over the country by clipping service companies or clipping bureaus to locate information printed in newspapers and magazines. Although most clipping services do not normally hire freelance readers, I've included this job in this book because it is a legitimate reading job you might be interested in pursuing. No special skill or training is necessary and no additional work, such as report writing, is required. If you like to get paid just to read articles and news items, this job may be of interest to you.

Clipping service readers are employed to read periodicals, looking for items of interest to the bureau's clients. When an article is found, it is clipped out and sent to the client. Some clipping service companies produce their own publications. They collect articles on specific topics, which are then reprinted as a collection and sold to subscribers.

Corporations, associations, nonprofit organizations, and individuals use clipping services for various reasons. These reasons could be to locate sales leads, monitor competition, check trademark infringements, keep abreast of their public image, or track the response of their publicity efforts. Many businesses subscribe to clipping service publications to detect new trends and changing attitudes of the population.

A primary source of information for newspaper and magazine articles is generated from news releases. Businesses send out news releases and other promotional materials throughout the country, describing new products, accomplishments, and other aspects about the company in order to get publicity or generate good public relations. Publicity increases business, keeps the company name in customers' minds, and builds a good image. Newspapers and magazines use news releases to report on what's happening. It is impossible for newspaper editors to know everything that is happening, so they depend on news releases for a good portion of the material they report. It is estimated that about 20-40 percent of the news in newspapers comes from news releases.

If a news release interests a reporter, he will use it to write an article. The article will publicize the business or organization and often provide useful comments that the businesses or organizations can use in future advertising or promotional efforts. For example, review copies of books are sent with news releases, a good book review will provide a publisher with an endorsement he can use in his advertising literature, and even on the book itself. For this reason, businesses and organizations like to collect as many news clippings and reviews as they can. Newspapers, however, do not normally send copies of the articles they write to the people they get the news releases from, nor do they even inform them that the news release resulted in an article. So, in order to gather clippings, the companies and individuals must have people reading all the newspapers. This is too much of a burden for most companies to do, so they hire a clipping service to do it for them.

Since the clipping bureau will have several clients and will be searching for many different topics, it would be impossible to keep track without a computer data base. When the reader comes across a person or topic that may be of interest, he will look up the name or topic in the computer. If the subject is listed, the article is marked and sent to the clipping department, where it is clipped, sorted, and eventually delivered to the client.

While most clipping service companies are confined to large metropolitan areas, they do have many regional offices throughout the country. The largest clipping bureaus are Bacon's Clipping Bureau, Burrelle's Press Clipping Service, International Press Clipping Bureau Inc., Luce Press Clippings, Newsclip Inc., NewsBank, Facts on File, and Marpep Publishing (Canada). The latter three services mentioned specialize in gathering news on specific topics and republishing it. For further information about clipping services, look in your phone book under "Clipping Bureaus" or "Press Clipping" and look in the "Business-to-Business" Yellow Pages. *Literary Market Place* also contains a listing of clipping bureaus.

ARTICLE READERS

Many publications will pay readers for finding interesting articles in local newspapers and magazines that can be reprinted nationally in their publication. *Reader's Digest,* for example, will pay up to $300 to the first person who sends in an article from a local publication which is "exceptionally heartwarming" and is reprinted in their magazine. Many other national consumer magazines do the same.

Not all magazines or newspapers will pay readers for finding interesting articles. You must find those publications which do. Usually, they will indicate this need somewhere in the magazine. Almost always when an article is reprinted in this manner, the publication will include a statement about their willingness to pay readers for similar articles.

If you are already a regular reader of these magazines, you know the type of articles they publish. Any article you submit to them must be similar to those they publish. That is to say, don't send an article about dogs to a cat magazine. No matter how great the article may be, it won't be accepted if it doesn't fit the publication's readership. If you are aware of publications that offer to buy reprints, keep their needs in mind as you read your local newspaper and regional magazines.

If you subscribe to or read many local or regional publications, your chances of finding appropriate articles will increase. You need not subscribe to all of the publications in your area. Libraries usually subscribe to publications, many of which are local. You can read these without purchasing a subscription.

The chances for making much money this way are limited. I have included article readers in this book to let you know that at least this opportunity exists. You won't be able to make a career out of finding articles, but if you like to read and keep your eyes open, you may be lucky enough to make some easy cash occasionally.

BEWARE OF THE CON ARTIST

I am including this section in this book because in recent years the reading business has been invaded by con artists who will take advantage of unsuspecting people interested in becoming freelance readers. In order to prevent you from falling prey to these vultures, I will describe their tactics so you can avoid embarrassment and financial loss. Hopefully, if enough people are aware of these practices, they will not continue.

One opportunity for con artists stems from the fact that book publishers are buried in unsolicited manuscripts. They cannot possibly spend the time to read each one thoroughly, so some book publishers employ freelance readers or first readers to read unsolicited manuscripts.

In publishing companies, most first readers are hired as employees and the job is usually at the entry level position for those seeking to become editors. They are not freelancers. However, a few publishing companies, literary agents, and others do hire qualified freelance manuscript readers to evaluate manuscripts for them. Getting this type of job, however, is not easy.

The idea of getting paid to read a manuscript is an enticing idea. Con artists have used this idea in their mail order scams. They advertise that anybody can become a publisher's reader and earn huge amounts of money reading manuscripts and writing brief book reviews or summaries. Publishers, they claim, overloaded with manuscripts, are eager to hire freelance readers to ease their workload. Potential customers are coerced into buying cheaply made how-to booklets or minidirectories, listing the names of publishers who supposedly hire readers. Many of these directories contain only a few pages and sell for as much $40. How-to booklets may sell for as much as $50. You can almost guarantee that any mail order source on this subject selling at prices this high are scams. *If the book is not available in your library or bookstore, you should think twice before buying it, especially if it costs more than $20.*

Publishers are not going to pay just anybody to evaluate manuscripts for them. The reader must have some qualifications. Most publishers or agents do not hire freelance manuscript readers, and there is no directory in existence that lists publishers who do. Our company has unfortunately been included in some of these directories that supposedly hire freelance manuscript readers. We do not use manuscript readers and never have. Yet, we've received hundreds of requests for employment from people conned by this scam. Beware and do not throw your money away on worthless directories or bogus how-to booklets. These types of materials, although not illegal, are misleading and of little value. The information you receive in this book is accurate and far more detailed and reliable than what you will get from these questionable, grossly overpriced sources.

These con artists advertise in newspapers and magazines, offering a money-making opportunity, at home, for reading books. The only real way you could make money at home reading books and manuscripts is through the methods described in this book.

Another scam involving freelance readers is with clipping services. Unlike the clipping service described earlier in this chapter, it is more similar to the description of an article reader, although some con artists may combine aspects of both clipping services and articles reading as a greater enticement.

The con artist entices people with the lure of working at home reading newspapers and magazines, claiming that publications all over the country are looking for articles to reprint. All you have to do is clip out interesting articles and send them to the prospective buyers. Publications, you are told, are eager to get clippings and will pay $25 or more for each article sent to them. Well, it is true that many publications will pay for appropriate articles, however, most do not. So in order to find publications who are willing to buy clippings, the con artist provides a directory, supposedly listing all these publications. All you have to do is buy the directory. Like the scam with manuscript readers described above, the directory costs $20 to $40 or more and consists of only a few pages and is totally fraudulent or at best misleading.

The idea of providing people with resources or directories where they can get something or sell something is a favorite game with con artists. Many business opportunities offered in classified ads use this concept to deceive the public. They use a legitimate practice and offer to sell a directory or how-to instructions to cash in on the opportunity. The advantages and opportunities of being a freelance reader are enticing to many people, but unfortunately, this is just the type of opportunity con artists like to capitalize on. Be very leery of buying any type of directory or list of companies who will pay for your reading services. To my knowledge none exist, and I do not believe one can even be created since needs of companies are continually changing. You need to build your own personal list of clients as described in Chapter 4.

APPENDIX

RESOURCES

ASSOCIATIONS AND ORGANIZATIONS

Membership in an appropriate organization can help you learn more about the profession, enable you to interact and network with other working professionals, and provide avenues which will enhance job opportunities.

American Home Business
Association
397 Post Road
Darien, CT 06820

American Library Association
50 E. Huron Street
Chicago, IL 60611

American Literary Translators
Association
University of Texas-Dallas
Box 830688
Richardson, TX 75083

American Mail Order Association
444 Lincoln Blvd., Suite 107
Venice, CA 90291

American Society for Information
Science
8720 Georgia Avenue, Suite 501
Silver Spring, MD 20910

American Society of Indexers
1700 18th Street NW
Washington, DC 20009

American Translators Association
109 Croton Avenue
Ossining, NY 10562

Association of Author's
Representatives
10 Astor Place, 3rd Floor
New York, NY 10003

Association of Editorial Businesses
4600 Duke Street
Alexandria, VA 22304

Authors Guild
234 W. 44th Street
New York, NY 10036

Direct Marketing Association
11 W. 42nd Street
New York, NY 10036

Editorial Freelancers Association
P.O. Box 2050
Madison Square Station
New York, NY 10159

Freelance Editorial Association
P.O. Box 835
Cambridge, MA 02238

Freelance Network
P.O. Box 36838
Miracle Mile Station
Los Angeles, CA 90036

Indexing and Abstracting Society
of Canada
P.O. Box 744, Sta. F
Toronto, Ontario M4Y 2N6
Canada

International Reading Association
P.O. Box 8139
Newark, DE 19714

Literary Translators Association of
Canada
1030 rue Cherrier, Bureau 510
Montreal, Quebec H2L 1H9
Canada

Mothers' Home Business Network
P.O. Box 423
East Meadow, NY 11554

National Association for the Self-
Employed
2328 Gravel Road
Ft. Worth, TX 76118

National Association of the
Cottage Industry
P.O. Box 14460
Chicago, IL 60614

National Association of Home
Based Businesses
P.O. Box 30220
Baltimore, MD 21270

National Association of Science
Writers
P.O. Box 294
Greenlawn, NY 11740

National Federation of Abstracting and Information Services
1429 Walnut Street, 13th Floor
Philadelphia, PA 19102

National Mail Order Association
3875 Wilshire Blvd., Suite 604
Los Angeles, CA 90010

National Writers Union
13 Astor Place
New York, NY 10003

Writer's Guild of America (East)
555 W. 57th Street
New York, NY 10019

Writer's Guild of America (West)
8955 Beverly Blvd.
Los Angeles, CA 90048

Writers' Union of Canada
24 Ryerson Ave.
Toronto, Ontario M5T 2P3
Canada

MAILING LIST COMPANIES

The companies listed here are just a few which offer mailing lists. The quality of mailing lists varies greatly from one company to another. I have listed some of the largest and most reliable companies. There are many other companies which sell mailing lists, some of which are almost worthless. For additional sources for reputable list companies ask your local librarian.

Best Mailing Lists, Inc.
38 West 32nd Street
New York, NY 10001

Cahners Direct Mail Services
1350 East Touhy Avenue
Des Plaines, IL 60018

Dunhill International List Co., Inc.
1100 Park Central Blvd., South
Pompano Beach, FL 33064

Hugo Dunhill Mailing Lists, Inc.
630 Third Avenue
New York, NY 10017

Mailings Clearing House
601 E. Marshall Street
Sweet Springs, MO 65351

Dunn & Bradstreet
International Services
99 Church Street
New York, NY 10007

Qualified Lists Corporation
135 Bedford Road
Armon, NY 10504

R.L. Polk & Co.
6400 Monroe Blvd.
Taylor, MI 48180

List Services Corporation
890 Ethan Allen Highway
Ridgefield, CT 06877

MAGAZINES FOR WRITERS AND PUBLISHERS

These publications are beneficial for learning more about the writing trade and how to get published, as well as developing skills as a reader. They also provide a source for obtaining customers through classified advertising, renting mailing lists, and networking.

Book Dealers World
North American Bookdealers
Exchange
P.O. Box 606
Cottage Grove, OR 97424

Byline
P.O. Box 130596
Edmond, OK 73013

Canadian Author & Bookman
Canadian Authors Association
121 Avenue Rd. Suite 104
Toronto, Ontario M5R 2G3
Canada

Canadian Writer's Journal
Gordon M. Smart Publications
P.O. Box 6618, Depot 1
Victoria, BC V8P 5N7
Canada

Editor & Publisher
11 W. 19th Street
New York, NY 10011

The Editorial Eye
Editorial Experts, Inc.
66 Canal Center Plaza, Suite 200
Alexandria, VA 22314

The Editors' Forum
Editors' Forum Publishing Co.
P.O. Box 411806
Kansas City, MO 64141

Freelance Writer's Report
Cassell Communications Inc.
P.O. Box 94844
Fort Lauderdale, FL 33310

Housewife-Writer's Forum
P.O. Box 780
Lyman, WY 82937

Magazine Issues
Feredonna Communications
Drawer 9890
Knoxville, TN 37940

New Writer's Magazine
Sarasota Bay Publishing
P.O. Box 5976
Sarasota, FL 34277

Publishers Weekly
249 West 17th Street
New York, NY 10011

Righting Words
Feredonna Communications
Drawer 9808
Knoxville, TN 37940

Scavenger's Newsletter
519 Ellinswood
Osage City, KS 66523

Science Fiction Chronicle
P.O. Box 2730
Brooklyn, NY 11202

Small Press
Small Press Inc.
Colonial Hill, RFD #1
Mt. Kisco, NY 10549

The Writer
120 Boylston St.
Boston, MA 02116

Writers Connection
1601 Saratoga-Sunnyvale Rd.,
Suite 180
Cupertino, CA 95014

Writer's Digest
F & W Publications, Inc.
1507 Dana Avenue
Cincinnati, OH 45207

Writer's Forum
F & W Publications, Inc.
1507 Dana Avenue
Cincinnati, OH 45207

Writer's Journal
Minnesota Ink, Inc.
27 Empire Drive
St. Paul, MN 55103

Writer's Nook News
38114 3rd Street, #181
Willoughby, OH 44904

INFORMATION SERVICES

The following computer information services are useful for researchers, book reviewers, writers, and others who have a personal computer and a modem.

CompuServe
5000 Arlington Center Blvd.
Columbus, OH 43220
800/848-8199

Dow Jones News Retrieval
Box 300
Princeton, NJ 08543
800/522-3567

The Knowledge Index
3460 Hillview Ave.
Palo Alto, CA 94304
800/334-2564

Prodigy
500 S. Broad St.
Meriden, CT 06450
800/776-3449

MARKETING AND BUSINESS RESOURCES

The following books will help you develop your business and market your services as a freelance reader and help you find markets for your services.

The Complete Guide to Editorial Freelancing, by Carol L. O'Neill and Avima Ruder (Dodd, Mead). A helpful guide for freelance editors, proofreaders, and writers.

Direct Mail Copy That Sells, by Herschell Gordon Lewis (Prentice-Hall). Techniques for writing advertising copy.

Direct Mail Magic: A Practical Guide to Effective Direct Mail Advertising, by Charles Mallory (Crisp Publishing). Describes how to sell through mail order marketing.

Getting Publicity: A Do-It-Yourself Guide for Small Business and Non-Profit Groups, by Tana Fletcher and Julia Rockler (Self-Counsel Press). Practical techniques for publicizing a small business.

Going Freelance: A Guide for Professionals, by Robert Laurance (John Wiley and Sons). A reference source for any type of freelance business.

Guide to Literary Agents and Art/Photo Reps, (Writer's Digest Books). An annual directory of literary agents and art and photo representatives.

Help for Your Growing Homebased Business, by Barbara Brabec (Barbara Brabec Productions). A helpful guide for people who have home-based businesses.

Home-Based Mail Order: A Success Guide for Entrepreneurs, by William J. Bond (Liberty House). Covers the basics of mail order marketing.

Homemade Money, by Barbara Brabec (Betterway Publications). An excellent resource book on how to start and operate a home-based business.

How to Create Small-Space Newspaper Advertising That Works, by Ken Eichenbaum (Unicom Publishing Group). A guide to writing effective newspaper advertisements.

How to Start and Run a Writing & Editing Business, by Herman Holtz (John Wiley & Sons). A basic introduction to the business of editorial freelancing.

Literary Agents: A Writer's Guide, by Debby Mayer (Poets & Writer's). A directory of agents which is published every five years.

Literary Agents of North America: The Complete Guide to U.S. and Canadian Literary Agencies, (Author Aid/Research Associates International). A directory of literary agents.

Literary Market Place, (R.R. Bowker). An annual directory which includes publishers, agents, reviewers, editorial services, magazines, newspapers, book clubs, indexing services, desktop publishing services, translators, clipping bureaus, and other businesses and services in the book publishing industry.

Mail Order Selling: How to Market Almost Anything by Mail, by Irving Burstiner (Prentice-Hall). Techniques of selling by mail order.

Mail Order Selling Made Easier: A Step-By-Step Guide to Organizing and Carrying Out a Successful Direct Marketing Program, by John Kremer (Open Horizons Publishing Company). An in-depth guide to mail order marketing.

Money in Your Mailbox, by L. Perry Wilbur (John Wiley & Sons). A good basic text on mail order marketing.

Novel and Short Story Writer's Market, edited by Robin Gee (Writer's Digest Books). An annual directory of book and magazine publishers interested in publishing fiction.

The Secrets of Practical Marketing for Small Business, by Herman Holtz (Prentice-Hall). An overview of various marketing techniques useful for small businesses.

Selling Your Services: Proven Strategies for Getting Clients to Hire You or Your Firm, by Robert W. Bly (Henry Holt and Company). Marketing techniques for service businesses.

Small-Time Operator, by Bernard Kamoroff (Bell Springs Publishing). An excellent text on how to start and operate a small business.

Translation and Translators: An International Directory and Guide, by Stefan Congrat-Butler (R. R. Bowker). A directory of translators and translation services.

Writer's Market, edited by Mark Kissling (Writer's Digest Books). An annual directory of book and magazine publishers.

Writing Effective News Releases: How to Get Free Publicity for Yourself, Your Business, or Your Organization, by Catherine V. McIntyre (Piccadilly Books). A valuable reference for getting free publicity through news releases.

READING RESOURCES

These books will help you improve your knowledge about the reading services described in this book. These are just a few of the many good books available to professional readers. For additional books check with your local library or bookstore.

The Art of Editing, by Floyd K. Baskette, Jack Z. Sissors, and Brian S. Brooks (Macmillam). Provides the basics of editing.

Be a Better Reader, by Nila Banton Smith (Prentice-Hall). A basic guide to help readers improve comprehension and reading skills.

A Beginner's Guide to Getting Published, by Kirk Polking (Writer's Digest Books). A good reference on how to sell your writing.

Beyond the Bestseller: A Literary Agent Takes You Inside the Book Business, by Richard Curtis (New American Library). An interesting look inside the book publishing business.

The Chicago Manual of Style, (University of Chicago Press). A valuable detailed reference on the elements of style for writers, editors, proofreaders, reviewers, indexers, translators, and others.

The Complete Book of Scriptwriting, by J. Michael Straczyniski (Writer's Digest Books). Describes how to write and sell all types of scripts.

The Complete Guide to Standard Script Format (Parts 1 and 2), by Hillis Cole and Judith Haag (CMC Publishing). A basic text on preparing scripts for scriptwriters and agents.

The Dramatists Sourcebook, edited by Angela E. Mitchell and Gilliam Richards (Theatre Communications Group). A directory of companies who buy scripts and also includes a listing of agents.

The Elements of Editing: A Modern Guide for Editors and Journalists, by Arthur Plotnik (Macmillian). A basic guide to editing.

The Elements of Grammar, by Margaret Shertzer (Macmillian). A simple guide to grammar.

The Elements of Style, by William Strunk, Jr. and E.B. White (Macmillian). A basic guide to elements of literary style.

The Everyday English Handbook, by Leonard Rosen (Dell Publishing). A basic text on proper English usage.

Handbook for Proofreading, by Laura K. Anderson (VGM Career Horizons). An excellent text on the principles of proofreading.

Handbook of Short Story Writing, edited by Frank Dickson, Sandra Smythe, and Jean M. Fredette (Writer's Digest Books). Describes how to create and sell short stories.

How to Get Your Book Published, by Herbert W. Bell (Writer's Digest Books). A basic guide to getting a book published.

How to Pitch and Sell Your TV Script, by David Silver (Writer's Digest Books). Information and techniques useful for author and agent on selling television scripts.

How to Read a Book: A Classic Bestselling Guide to Reading Books and Accessing Information, by Mortimer Adler and Charles Van Doren (Donald I. Fine, Inc.). Teaches how to analyze books, comprehend structure, dissect its main argument, and consider its bias.

How to Read a Page: A Course in Efficient Reading, by I. A. Richards (Beacon Press). A guide to improving reading skills.

How to Understand and Negotiate a Book Contract or Magazine Agreement, by Richard Balkin (Writer's Digest Books). A valuable guide to understanding publishing contracts for writers and agents.

How to Write a Book Proposal, by Michael Larsen (Writer's Digest Books). Explains how to prepare a professional book proposal for publishers and agents.

How to Write Irresistible Query Letters, by Lisa Collier Cool (Writer's Digest Books). Describes how to write effective query letters to publishers and agents.

How You Can Make $25,000 a Year Writing, by Nancy Edmonds Hanson (Writer's Digest Books). An interesting guide to getting published.

Knowing Where to Look, by Lois Horowitz (Writer's Digest Books). An excellent reference book on how to do research.

Lincoln's Doctor's Dog and Other Famous Best Sellers, by George Stevens (J.B. Lippincott Co.). An entertaining account of how books become best sellers.

The Literary Agent and the Writer: A Professional Guide, by Diane Cleaver (Writer's Digest Books). Written for writers on how to find and work with literary agents.

Literary Agents: How to Get and Work with the Right One for You, by Michael Larsen (Writer's Digest Books). How to select, approach, and work with agents.

The Magazine Article: How to Think It, Plan It, Write It, by Peter Jacobi (Writer's Digest Books). The basics of writing good magazine articles.

Mark My Words, by Peggy Smith (Editorial Experts). Excellent text on proofreading and copyediting, includes many practice exercises.

The Modern Researcher, by Jacques Barzun (Harcourt Brace Jovanovich). A text on the methods used in researching.

Pinckert's Practical Grammar, by Robert C. Pinckert (Writer's Digest Books). Basics of English grammar.

Proofreading and Copyediting, by Harry H. McNaughton (Hastings House). Techniques and skills used in proofreading and copyediting.

Reading for a Living: How to Be a Professional Story Analyst for Film and Television, by T.L. Katahn (Blue Arrow Books). A detailed text on working as a story analyst in the film industry.

Reference Readiness: A Manual for Librarians, Researchers, and Students, by Agnes Ann Hede (Library Professional Publications). A reference source for researchers.

A Short Guide to Writing a Critical Review, by Eliot D. Allen and Ethel B. Colbrunn (Everett/Edwards). A useful aid for book reviewers.

The TV Scriptwriter's Handbook, by Alfred Brenner (Writer's Digest Books). Information on the movie and television business, as well as preparing and selling scripts.

Translate to Communicate: A Guide for Translators, by Mary Massound (David C. Cook Foundation). An introduction to the art of translating.

Use Your Foreign Language!: Creative Ideas for Effectively Using Your Foreign Language Skills in Today's World of Opportunities, by Raymond G. Scheuerman (Bilingual Communication Service). A short text describing many opportunities for translators.

Writer's Digest Guide to Manuscript Formats, by Dian Dincin Buchman and Seli Groves (Writer's Digest Books). A comprehensive guide to preparing manuscripts for publishers and agents.

Writer's Digest Handbook of Magazine Article Writing, edited by Jean Fredette (Writer's Digest Books). A comprehensive guide to magazine article writing.

A Writer's Guide to Contract Negotiations, by Richard Balkin (Writer's Digest Books). A valuable guide to understanding and negotiating a publishing contract.

The Writer's Survival Manual, by Carol Meyer (Crown Publishers). A guide to getting published.

Writing A to Z, edited by Kirk Polking, Joan Bloss, Colleen Cannon, and Debbie Cinnamon (Writer's Digest Books). A helpful aid on improving writing skills.

Writing Book Reviews, by John E. Drewry (Greenwood Press Publishers). An introduction to writing good book reviews.

The Writing Business, by Donald MacCampbell (Crown Publishers). A good resource on writing and how to get published.

Writing Scripts That Sell, by Michael Hauge (McGraw-Hill). Techniques of writing good scripts, useful for writers and agents.

Writing with Precision: How to Write So That You Cannot Possibly be Misunderstood, by Jefferson D. Bates (Acropolis Books). Techniques of good writing.

INDEX

Accuracy, 50-51
Adler, Mortimer, 186
Advances, 164
Advertising
  classified, 36-37
  direct mail, 37-39
  flyers, 35
  phone book, 149, 167
  sales package, 39
A Handbook for Literary Translators,
  148
American Association of Language
  Specialists, 152
American Film Institute, 186
American Literary Translators
  Association, 152
American Society for Information
  Science, 161
American Society of Indexers, 161
American Translators
  Associantion, 20, 56, 151-152
Artical reader, 23, 190-191
Association of Authors'
  Representatives, 174
Association of Editorial Businesses,
  113

Balkin, Richard, 173
Billing and collections, 29-30
Book clubs, 177
Book evaluations, 179
Booklist, 127
Book proposals, 168-72
Book reviewing, 18, 115-29
Books, as a research tool, 135
Books in Print, 128, 183
Brabec, Barbara, 31-32
Brochures, 48
Businesses, 14
Business
  address, 26-27
  bank account, 27
  cards, 35
  license, 26
  name, 25-26
  records, 28-29
  stationary, 27-28

Business Use of Your Home, 28
Byline, 61, 80

CIA, 141, 145
*CIS/Index and Abstracts to Publica-
  tions of the U.S. Congress, 139*
Cheshire labels, 38
Chicago Manual of Style, The, 90-91,
  160
CompuServe, 139
Con artists, 191-93
Copyediting, 16, 102-10
Copyright, 79, 94
Cover letter, 40-44, 169
Coverages, 177
Cox, Kerry, 174
Clipping bureaus, 188, 190
Clipping service companies, *see*
  Clipping bureaus
Clipping service reader, 22-23, 188-
  190
Clips, 47, 60, 127, 189, *see also*
  Publishing credits
Criticism fee, 166
Cross-reference, 155, 158

Daily Variety, 174
Dead copy, 88
Deadlines, 51-53
Department of State, 145
Division of Language Services, 145
Dictionaries, 136, 137-38
Dow Jones News Retrieval, 139
Dry reading, 88

Editorial Freelancers Association, 113
Editorial style, 90-94
  abbreviations, 92
  capitalization, 91
  dates, 92
  foreign words, 93
  hyphenation, 91
  numerals, 92
  plurals, 92
  possessives, 92
  servicemarkes, 94
  spelling, 91
  tables and graphs, 94
  trademarks, 94

Endorsements, 44
Educators, as clients, 13
Encyclopedias, 137

Fact checkers, 131
FBI, 141, 146
Fictitious name statement, 25
Film producers, 147, 173, 184
First readers, 22, 176, 177
Flush-and-hang, 157

Galley, 68, 154
Genealogy, 132, 134
Government, 14
Government documents, 138
Guide to Literary Agents and Art/Photo Reps, 175, 185

Help for Your Growing Homebased Business, 31
Hollywood Reporter, The, 174
Hollywood Scriptwriter, The, 174
Homemade Money, 31
Horowitz, Lois, 140
How to Read a Book, 186
How to Sell Your Screenplay, 174
How to Understand and Negotiate a Book Contract or Magazine Agreement, 173
Huge, Michael, 174

Indented, 157, 158
Indexes, as a research tool, 137-38
Indexing, 20, 153-61
Indexing and Abstracting Society of Canada, 161
Indicia, 123
International Reply Coupon (IRC), 83

Joint Publications Research Service (JPRS), 145, 146
Journalism, 116

Kamoroff, Bernard, 32
Katahn, T.L., 186
Kill fee, 69
Kirkus Reviews, 127

Knowing Where to Look, 140
Knowledge Index, The, 139

Larsen, Michael, 175
Lawyers, 144
Letter of agrement, 30, 54, 163
Libraries, 132-35
  academic, 133
  government, 133
  historical and museum, 134
  public, 133
  private, 134
Library Journal, 127
Library science, 19, 139, 161
Literary agents, 20-21, 162-75
Literary Agents: A Writers Guide, 175
Literary Agents: How to Get and Work with the Right One for You, 175
Literary Agents of North America, 175
Literary critizism, 17, 110-13
Literary Market Place, 12, 38, 124, 175, 190
Literary services, 85-113
Live copy, 88

Magazine
  article reading, 190
  article writing, 62, 72
  as a research tool, 136
  consumer, 60
  editors, working with, 67-70
  publishing, 48, 59
  readership, 65-66, 118
  trade, 60, 118, 136
Mail
  bulk, 38
  lists, 37
  postage, 28
  postal boxes, 26
Making a Good Script Great, 174
Manuscript
  preparation, 76-80
  reading, 22, 176-86
  submissions, 80, 83-84, 171
Marketing, 33-49

Marketing fees, 165, 166
Mayer, Debby, 175
Monthly Catalog, 139
Microfiche, 139
Movie producers, *see* Film producers

National Federation of Abstracting
    and Information Services, 161
National Home Business Report, 32
Newspaper, 116, 136, 188
News release, 123, 129, 189
Non-profit organizations, 15
*Novel and Short Story Writer's
    Market*, 163
"Nuisance" lawsuits, 174

Outline, 169, 170

Pay-on-publication, 70
Personal computers, 78, 139, 154
Photos, 84
Prepublication reviews, 127
Press release, *see* News release
Prodigy, 139
Production companies, *see* Film
    producers
Proofreader's marks, 97, 99-102
Proofreading, 16, 86-102
Pseudonym, 79
Publishers, 11-12, 13, 147, 184
Publishers Weekly, 127, 128
Publishing agreements, 172-73
Publishing credits, 44, 47, 57, 58

Query letters, 63, 72-76

Rates, 53-55
Reader's Digest, 190
*Reader's Guide to Periodical
    Literature*, 138
Reading for a Living, 186
Reading fees, 165
Reference books, 136
Researching, 18, 130-40
Resume, 44, 45-46
Royalty, 164
Run-in, 157

Sales letter, 72, *see also* Cover letter
Sautter, Carl, 174
Seger, Linda, 174
Self-publishing, 12
Screenplays, 178
Script agents, 173
Slug line, 80
Slush pile, 169-170
Small publications, 61, 85, 161
Small-Time Operator, 32
Smith, Peggy, 113
Spanish, 150, 151
Spelling, 95-98
Story analysts, 177
Student reader, 22, 187-88
Students, as clients, 13
Style sheet, 91
Subject Guide to Books in Print, 137
Successful Scriptwriting, 174
Synopsis, 169, 170

Talent agents, 184
Taxes, 28-29
Tax Guide for Small Business, 28
Technical reading, 17, 110
Television producers, *see* Film
    producers
Textbooks, 186
Translating, 19, 141-52
Translating bureaus, 149
Translator Training Guidelines, 152
Travel agents, 143

U.S. Information Agency, 146

Van Doren, Charles, 186

Wolff, Jurgen, 174
Writers, as clients, 12-13
Writers' and Artists' Yearbook, 175
Writers Guild of America (WGA),
    173, 174
Writer's Market, 12, 36, 38, 55, 60,
    64, 124, 163
Writing credits, *see* Publishing credits
Writing Screen Plays That Sell, 174
Writing tips, 70